Building Economics and Cost Control

Worked solutions

A. Ashworth MSc ARICS
Senior Lecturer in Quantity Surveying, Preston Polytechnic

Butterworths
London Boston Durban Singapore Sydney Toronto Wellington

First published 1983

© Butterworth & Co (Publishers) Ltd 1983

British Library Cataloguing in Publication Data

Ashworth, Allan
  Building economics and cost control.
  1. Building – Estimates – Great Britain –
  Problems, exercises, etc.   2. Building –
  Cost control – Problems, exercises, etc.
  I. Title
  690′068′1   TH435

  ISBN 0-408-01353-2

Photoset by Butterworths Litho Preparation Department
Printed in Great Britain by Page Bros. Ltd., Norwich, Norfolk

Contents

Preface

Building economics and cost control has become a particularly important subject to study within the discipline of quantity surveying, and is also given some consideration by both designers and contractors. It seeks to ensure the efficient use of available resources in the construction industry.

There are already several excellent books which describe and detail the subjects of building economics, cost planning and cost control applicable to the construction industry. There is also further supporting information and literature that is available to both practitioners and students alike. There are, however, few textbooks dealing with worked solutions to practical examination problems, yet such books are of particular value and interest to students. Furthermore, questions taken from previous examinations of appropriate professional institutions are even more relevant. However, the contents of this book provide only for worked solutions to the problems posed. They are not intended to be the only solution available or a model answer, but are intended to cover the main points relevant to the discussion.

The idea for this book originated from a series of questions written by the author for 'QS Weekly', a news magazine for quantity surveyors. These articles received an enthusiastic response, both from the then editor Mr William Pike and also from many students who found the series useful, informative and helpful in their revision. Although some of the examples were previously printed in 'QS Weekly', many of the questions are entirely new. This book also includes many examples which, because of their length, are unsuitable for publication in a weekly periodical.

The book is of particular relevance to quantity surveyors, although students of other disciplines, e.g. building surveyors, who need to study this subject will also find it useful. It is, therefore, appropriate to students studying for the RICS (quantity surveying division), IQS, CSI and CIOB examinations.

Students reading for quantity surveying degrees or studying on diploma courses will find the book helpful in their learning process. It will also be a useful reference book to students of the other professions of architecture, building and civil engineering particularly where construction economics is part of their course.

I am grateful to the Institute of Quantity Surveyors, the Royal Institution of Chartered Surveyors and Preston Polytechnic for granting me permission to reproduce their examination questions. I would also like to express my thanks for being able to quote from the Building Cost Information Service.

Finally, I would like to thank Frances Dewar for her care in typing the manuscript.

A. Ashworth,
Preston 1982

1 Construction economics

The construction industry is sometimes used by the government as an economic regulator.

(1) Discuss how government can implement such a policy.
(2) Discuss the effect it has on
   (a) the national economy.
   (b) the construction industry.

(1) The importance of the construction industry in the economy is due to three factors:

   (a) Its size. In the early 1970s the value of building in the United Kingdom amounted to 12 per cent of the gross domestic product. The labour force employed was in the region of 6 per cent. The number employed in the repair and maintenance section alone is greater than that in agriculture, coal mining, shipbuilding and many other large industries.
   (b) It provides predominantly investment goods. Construction is an investment industry; its products are wanted not for their own sake but for the goods or services which they can help to create. This is particularly true for factory buildings, but it also applies to the majority of other building types.
   (c) Government is a large client. In the early 1970s public building accounted for over 50 per cent of the construction industry's workload. Work undertaken for local authorities, central government and public corporations falling into this category.

In managing the economy, the government has four main objectives:

   (i) The ability to pay its way abroad by balancing the payments.
   (ii) An acceptable level of employment of resources, particularly manpower.
   (iii) An increase in the amount of goods and services produced and consumed, leading to a rise in the standard of living.
   (iv) The control of inflation.

In spite of the damage to efficiency of sudden stops and starts in its workload, because of its size and importance the construction industry is a tempting regulator of the economy. Economists, however, are in some disagreement about whether the industry is ever used as such.

Government measures to control the economy usually affect the industry either directly or indirectly: by the control of output by increasing or reducing public expenditure, or by a restriction on borrowing via high interest charges.

1

(2)(a) The effects of changes in output, employment, incomes or demand in the construction industry are likely to have repercussions in other sectors of the economy. Thus a decline in construction activity will have an adverse effect on many other industries.

  (b) (i) Government has an important role because public authorities buy over half of its output.

   (ii) A steady rather than a wildly fluctuating workload is important if the industry is to plan and manage its resources properly.

   (iii) Government economic policy will either stimulate or depress the construction industry.

   (iv) The adverse effects of a depression on the construction industry are as follows:

- Unemployment of building operatives.
- Smaller firms being forced out of business.
- Large firms being reluctant to invest large sums of money in plant and equipment, or to experiment with new techniques.
- Suppliers of materials and components being unlikely to extend their plants.
- Recruitment of persons into the industry at all levels being made more difficult.
- Lack of continuity of work equals increased costs and reduced efficiency.

What is meant by the term construction economics?

Construction economics is a branch of general economics. It consists of the application of the techniques and expertise of economics to the particular area of the construction industry. Economics, in general, is about the choice of the way in which scarce resources are and ought to be allocated between all their possible uses. Construction economics is concerned with man's needs for shelter and the suitable and appropriate conditions in which to live. It seeks to ensure the efficient use of available resources to the industry, and to increase the rate of growth of construction work in the most efficient manner. It includes a study of the following:

(1) A client's requirements. This involves a study of the client's wants and needs, and ensuring that the design of the project is kept within the available funds to be provided by the client. The client's requirements can be summarised as follows: satisfied that the building meets his needs, is available for occupation on the specified date for completion, the final account closely resembles the estimate and the construction project can be maintained at reasonable cost.

(2) The possible effects on the surrounding areas if the development is carried out. This considers the wider aspects associated with planning and the general amenities affected by proposed new construction projects.

(3) The relationship of space and shape. This evaluates the cost implications of the design variables, and considers those aspects of a particular design and their effects on cost. It does not seek to limit the architect's design skill or the aesthetic appearance of the project, but merely attempts to inform the architect and the client of the influence of their design on the overall cost.

(4) The assessment of the initial cost. This is the establishment of an initial estimate that is sufficiently accurate for advice purposes and which can be used for comparison purposes throughout the building process.

(5) The reasons for, and methods of, controlling costs. One of the client's main requirements for any construction project is the assessment of its expected cost. The methods used for controlling the costs will vary depending upon the type of project and the nature of the client. The methods adopted should be reasonably accurate, but flexible enough to suit the individual client's requirements.

(6) Estimating the life of buildings and materials. The emphasis on the initial construction costs has moved to consider the overall costs in use. The spending of a little more initially can result in a considerable saving over the life of the building. However, estimation of building-material life, interest rates and the economic life of a project can be difficult to determine in practice.

In addition, the wider economic aspects are worthy of note. These are:

(1) The role of the surveyors, engineers and builders employed in the industry.

(2) The division of the industry between the design and construction process.

(3) The size of the industry, its relationship to other industries and the national economy.

(4) The types of development undertaken.

(5) The types and sizes of construction firms, and the availability of specialist contractors.

(6) The variations in building costs and factors that influence these variations, such as market conditions, regional location etc.

The construction industry has characteristics which distinguish it from other industries. These can be classified as follows:

(1) The physical nature of the product.
(2) The structure of the industry.
(3) The organisation of the construction process.
(4) The method of price determination.

The final product is often large and expensive, and is required over a wide geographical area. Buildings and other structures are for the most part specially made to the requirements of each individual customer, although there is the provision for some speculative work, particularly in housing. The nature of the product also means that each contract often represents a large proportion of the work of a single contractor in any year, causing substantial discontinuity to the production functions.

Discuss the economic outlook for the construction industry over the next five years.

The answer to this question must largely be of a speculative nature, but nevertheless the following factors should be considered.

Government policy

Because government is a large client of the construction industry, any change in its policy towards new buildings or engineering projects is likely to have a considerable influence on the economic position of the industry. A reduction in housing, educational buildings, hospitals and the road-building programme will have serious effects on both the professions and the constructors. The trend has been to spend more upon the rehabilitation and maintenance of works in preference to new projects, although the actual amounts invested have been inadequate. Government policies in respect of tax concessions, development grants and interest rates have all influenced the contraction of the industry.

Industrial activity

Another major client of the construction industry is manufacturing industry. A reduced market both at home and overseas will only discourage industrialists from expansion into new or enlarged premises. The effect of a shrinking market has a knock-on effect on smaller manufacturers and other industries, with a consequent loss of possible new building schemes. This reduction in economic activity has a far-reaching effect, resulting in a lack of confidence generally on any possible future development.

World economic trends

A world recession affects particularly a country's exporting capabilities. This results in a reduced home base, which may increase costs and therefore prices charged, because of reduced economics of scale, resulting in further recession. This can only result in a decline for construction orders in many areas and types of work.

Political trends

The political influence of a government can have immense effects upon the economic outlook of the construction industry, and must never be underestimated. For example, a government committed to increased public expenditure in capital projects is likely to provide a considerable proportion of work for the industry. However, such a government may be more inclined to develop a public-building corporation or expand the direct labour organisations, which may thus provide mixed fortunes for the building industry. In the long term this may not directly benefit the private contractor. Because a large proportion of expertise lies in the private sector, this may mean the switching of allegiance of many of the industry's employees. An alternative political viewpoint may favour encouraging the private sector to expand at the expense of the public sector.

Energy sources

A large investment has been made in recent years in both the gas and oil industries. Nuclear energy has also been expanded. Research is currently being undertaken to find alternatives to rapidly diminishing fossil fuels and to nuclear power (which is fraught with political argument). Whatever energy sources are used, all involve the construction industry for capital projects.

Conservation

There has in recent years been an unprecedented attempt to conserve, repair or modernise premises. This has been particularly true in housing, where the emphasis has shifted away from new construction and towards the rehabilitation of existing properties. Considerable expertise has grown up around this work, and this sector of the construction industry is still increasing.

Changes in technology

The construction industry is today still very much a labour-intensive industry. Automation resulting in reduced labour forces in manufacturing industry has not been matched in the construction industry. System building, with components manufactured under factory conditions, has moved only a little way in this direction. Apart from speed of erection, this type of building has disadvantages in cost, function, appearance, life and recurring costs. Some changes in methods and materials used for construction are expected during the next decade. Mechanisation of the building site has made some inroads, but in future this may make an even greater impact.

Silicon chip

The chip has begun to affect the way we run our lives. This could have many diverse effects upon the construction industry, e.g. greater environmental control of buildings, further automation in materials manufacture and an influence in the way buildings are designed. The chip will also have far-reaching effects on the building professions, as we move towards an 'electronic office'.

Projects tend to be completed more quickly in the USA than in the United Kingdom. Suggest some of the underlying reasons for the poor performance of completion times in the UK.

There have been a number of comparisons between the US and UK construction industries over the past decade. Dramatic comparisons between the time taken to build Sears Tower in Chicago and the National Westminster Bank Tower in London, and the more serious studies by Slough Estates Ltd., are two examples. All the work arrives at the same conclusion: that the US construction industry produces buildings more quickly than the UK. The results of the earlier studies have caused many aspects of the UK approach to construction to be questioned. Often it has been assumed that there must be a single simple cause for the inferior UK performance.

There is, however, no general agreement on which factors are important and which are not. There is no established theoretical framework to guide the study, and the current level of understanding is not highly developed.

Some of the factors that might be considered when comparing building performance in these two countries are listed below. They are suggested in the report 'UK and US construction industries: a comparison of design and contract procedures' published by the RICS. They are not ranked in any order of importance.

It has been suggested by others that the real difference between the two countries is the absence of the quantity surveyor in the US, and his important role in the UK. Whilst this fact cannot be denied, someone in the US must, however, undertake 'quantity surveying' work. From these reports it is evident that the quantity surveyor is not one of the reasons for our poor performance. Indeed the report suggests that the US should consider employing quantity surveyors for the good of their construction industry.

A lengthy design process, the necessity for variations, higher standards of quality control, the delayed involvement of the contractor, restrictive labour practices, less mechanisation and a less predictable workload are probably some of the main reasons. These are now examined in greater detail.

(1) UK clients expect to be able to change their brief both during the design stage and whilst the construction work is being carried out on site. The US clients know that changes to the building during the construction phase are very expensive and offer poor value for money, and are generally discouraged. Changes to the contractor's work programme can be a major factor causing delay.

(2) UK orthodox procedures are largely determined by public sector insistence on control and accountability. The US procedures have to respond to private sector demands for speed, and a clear allocation of responsibilities and risks.

(3) Large technically advanced or risky projects are approached differently. The US clients are much more prepared to adopt unorthodox procedures.

(4) Any comparison of time and cost must also take into account the quality of the finished projects. In this respect, it can be argued that US buildings are inferior. For example, inaccuracies and tolerances in concrete work are much greater than in the UK.

(5) The UK construction industry is very much geared to refurbishment, which provides an attitude of 'make do and mend'. In the US, buildings decay and are then demolished. This latter approach of providing new buildings leads to both fast and cheap building performance.

(6) Although US buildings are constructed more quickly than UK ones, there is no significant difference between the total construction costs of office buildings in these two countries.

(7) The time taken for both the design and construction work is longer in the UK than in the US. A longer design period is often required in the UK in order to comply with the planning regulations.

(8) Office buildings in the UK provide more recreational and social amenities and therefore less actual office space than similar buildings in the US. The latter are also more intensively occupied than in the UK, so that the cost to the users is therefore less.

(9) Detailed design decisions have a very high impact on costs and time. The separation of design from construction always involves major time and cost penalties. The US system involves the contractor's influence at the design stage, when account can be taken of construction methods. The traditional UK system prevents this involvement.

(10) The incentives offered by the finance and tax structures in the US encourage the faster completion of buildings. The dominant philosophy in the industry is 'time is money'.

(11) Speed of construction in the US is achieved by different work practices from those in the UK. Many of these result from the willingness of US engineers and architects to accept alternative designs from the contractors and subcontractors, aimed at simplifying the building construction.

(12) There is a recognition in the US that wet trades in the building process will slow down progress. They are thus kept to an absolute minimum, and emphasis is placed upon simple methods of construction.

(13) The US construction worker does not physically work any harder or longer than the UK counterpart. The higher productivity is achieved partly through less complicated construction details and the use of more mechanical aids.

(14) Construction plant used in the US is generally larger than that in the UK, where greater emphasis is placed on selecting the smallest plant which is capable of doing the work. The tendency is partly due to the fact that transportation in the US is easier because of their much wider carriageways.

(15) Better welfare facilities are provided by UK contractors, and their safety record is much better than that of the US construction industry. Overtime in the US is unusual and incentive payments in the form of bonuses are not paid, owing to the higher hourly rates received by operatives. There is an ease of 'hire and fire' in the US construction industry, which alleviates the problems of the US contractor regarding resource levelling. US unions generally are contacted regarding the selection of appropriate labour. The unions' attitude is generally that if their construction industry is healthy, then their members will be employed, and they are prepared to adopt a flexible attitude to ensure that this is so.

(16) There is a more stable and predictable demand for construction in the US, and this provides for greater efficiency throughout the whole process of designing and work on site.

7

2   Cost control

'Cost control of a construction project is primarily the responsibility of the quantity surveyor'. Discuss.

The quantity surveying profession has gradually evolved over the past 100 years, although in more recent years there has been a rapid expansion of its services into new areas of work. 200 years ago architects were responsible not only for the design but also for the construction of the works in a more direct manner, and also for 'cost control'. In addition they often played an important role with engineering-type projects. Their overall importance, therefore, in the construction industry has diminished somewhat. Civil engineers used to accept (and regrettably some still do) that quantity surveyors were unnecessary. This stems largely from a misunderstanding of the work of the quantity surveyor and the work that he performs. Quantity surveyors, themselves, have often shown too much preopccupation with building projects at the expense of other types of work in the construction industry, and so have until recent years left cost control to ill-equipped architects, engineers and builders. Although these other members of the construction profession should be aware of the effect of their actions on construction costs, cost control should primarily be the province of the quantity surveyor.

The cost control of a construction project, or indeed any type of project, should start at the inception stage and not finish until the project is handed over to the client. Even then the final cost is still likely to be agreed, and there is scope for cost control of the recurring costs in use throughout the life of the building.

The following factors support the viewpoint that this area of responsibility is naturally that of the quantity surveyor.

(1) Architects and engineers tend to prefer design, investigation and construction. They are not generally interested in measurement, valuation and cost control.
(2) Engineers and architects are ill-equipped to deal with the complexities of cost control. Their training and education for this work is negligible and inadequate.
(3) Quantity surveyors are, by contrast, specially trained to ensure that clients obtain value for money, and that payments due are the correct amounts.

The efficient system of cost control in the building industry is due largely to the efforts of the quantity surveyor. The days of the addendum bill have largely disappeared, and where a project is adequately designed and documented, the problems of claims, accepted in certain quarters of the construction industry, should not occur. Even amidst mounting pressure and cynicism, the quantity surveyor has been one of the few professionals in the construction industry to show signs of continuing development.

The cost control of major building projects has long since been the territory of the quantity surveyor, and he has an even more important role to play in the administration and cost control of minor or small works projects. However, the quantity surveyor does not necessarily use the same techniques for different types of project, but adapts his methods and processes for the type and size of project under examination. In the area of package-deal projects (which are assumed to be increasing in number), a wise client is always likely to retain the services of the independent quantity surveyor, not only for cost advice but also cost control throughout the duration of the contract.

The quantity surveyor is also the more suitable person for the cost control of engineering projects, such as civil engineering, process plant engineering and mechanical services within buildings. The argument that is often used for retaining outdated and inefficient methods where they still occur, is that the majority of other countries appear to 'get by' without the quantity surveyor. In recent years, quantity surveying and cost control methods have been used more widely (where they were absent before) in countries like the USA and in Europe. They have for many years been employed in countries that are members of the British Commonwealth.

The argument that the quantity surveyor is really a cost advisor and does not in practice control costs is merely a play on words. Quantity surveying is seen as the profession that undertakes the function of cost control within the building industry. It could be argued that since the designer is responsible for issuing and approving variations, he dictates the amount of extra works, and looks to the quantity surveyor for cost advice and for cost records. On the other hand, there is the point that since the quantity surveyor prepares the valuations for interim payments, he controls the cash flow between client and contractor. It can also be reasonably argued that during the design process without the cost 'control' from the quantity surveyor the project could get financially out of hand, as often occurred before quantity surveyors developed cost planning. The same argument would be used in support of post-contract quantity surveying services.

'The cost control of engineering services in buildings is different from the approach applied to the other building elements'. Discuss this statement and comment upon the comparative cost efficiency of the services and building elements.

Engineering services in today's modern buildings often account for over 30 per cent of the initial project costs. The percentage is often considerably higher than this, as environmental control inside the building becomes an ever-increasing requirement in the design. As a direct consequence of this approach, the costs to the owner after completion of the construction contract will represent a substantial annual charge for running, repairs and replacement charges. These sums will represent a large proportion of the costs in use for the project.

Traditionally, engineering services are undertaken by specialist contractors, and are therefore often incorporated within bills of quantities as prime cost sums. The budgets required for the cost plans are provided by the engineering services consultant. The design and specification (performance specifications are sometimes used) would also be prepared by this consultant. Bills of quantities were, and still are, somewhat unusual. The preparation of any other contract documents, inviting quotations, assessing and selecting tenders would also be undertaken by the engineer. The quantity surveyor's traditional role was therefore to accept lump sums for inclusion in the bills, allow for interim payments and adjust the Prime Cost Sum in the final account by means of an invoice.

The quantity surveyor is therefore able to control costs effectively for only about 70 per cent of the project. It has been correctly suggested that because this work is sub-contracted, so too is the function of cost control. There has, needless to say, been some rivalry between the quantity surveyor and the services consultant as to who should undertake the cost control of engineering services.

The ability to control costs can be described as cost efficiency. The whole process of cost planning developed by the quantity surveying profession seeks to achieve this objective and its efficiency can be measured by the end product. A sum is allocated as a target for an element, and as the design develops the quantity surveyor can realistically cost this design and compare it with the element target cost. In this way the effects on the costs of alternative design solutions can be made. Alterations can, therefore, be made to the design before the building work is started, in order to avoid abortive designs and to restrict overspending.

Adopting the traditional system for engineering services, the engineer will predict sums for the various engineering services based upon previous projects and expected future needs. The work will not be properly or adequately cost-analysed, and therefore no appropriate cost control can be undertaken until the design is completed. This may mean that if the final design is too expensive, some redesign will be necessary, resulting in a less than satisfactory project. Without some detailed form of cost analysis, design within a cost target will be difficult to achieve. Cost control throughout the contract period is both minimal and unsatisfactory. Either the contractor is assumed to have included all that was required, extra work is paid for on the basis of some vague change in the specification, or alterations are made to the price of the work on an ad-hoc basis.

Because the engineering services represent such a large proportion of the whole contract, if the cost control of this section is inefficient, then the entire cost control function for the whole project becomes questionable. There is little real merit in properly controlling only 70 per cent of the contract value, if the remaining part is not also subject to stringent requirements and accountability.

A more modern approach is to employ the quantity surveyor to undertake full cost control functions for this work using his already proven system. This has already been the method adopted on some complex engineering services projects, where the quantity surveyor has either been employed in his own practice or in the office of an engineering consultant.

Discuss the importance of cost research to the profession of quantity surveying.

Cost research involves the examination of construction costs from any aspect either through the client's viewpoint or on the basis of the costs of a contractor's organisation. It also includes their effects on the economy and a development of the efficient use of resources. The purpose of such research is to develop a basic understanding that enables the planning, monitoring and controlling of all costs to be undertaken more effectively and with greater certainty.

Many quantity surveyors do not see research as a means of development either individually or for the profession in general. They are not alone in this opinion; it is shared by other professions within the construction and other industries. It stems from the fact that some research is done simply for its own sake, without any suggestion of useful practical application. But in even the best research projects, a large amount of research and investigation is needed to secure only a little progress. It is, however, generally accepted that research should be more carefully planned and monitored, and this would then secure greater advantages to the profession.

Cost research is carried out by many different sectors of the profession. A large proportion of research work has been undertaken by the universities and polytechnics, and the considerable increase in quantity surveying research is largely attributable to their staff. In addition, the professional institutions have adopted their own research programmes, often of direct application to the profession. However, the profession has not always been helpful in suggesting suitable topics for research, and there has always been resistance to change. Some professional practices have made significant contributions towards quantity surveying development, and several of the processes we now use are as a direct result of their ideas. Several government departments have also formulated their own research programmes to examine building cost aspects applicable to their own projects but often incorporating much wider applications. For example, within the Property Services Agency (PSA), a group named the Department of Quantity Surveying Services (DQSS) has, as part of its function, the investigation of the cost aspects of construction. There is also the valuable work of the Building Research Establishment (BRE), or the various trade associations who sometimes undertake cost studies as an aid to commercial expertise.

Accepting that research will be carried out, albeit by a minority of quantity surveyors, what advantages can the profession hope to achieve?

Science of quantity surveying

The majority of the other professions have been in existence much longer than that of quantity surveying. They have therefore been able to establish for themselves an academic basis of understanding of their subject knowledge. Some quantity surveying procedures have been accepted without the basic formulation of the principles involved. This is not meant as a direct criticism of the profession or to invalidate the procedures used, but the present position must be to substantiate the theories and accepted practices of the quantity surveyor's work.

Understanding

Understanding the economics of construction has been a new study, developing only during the past thirty years. The understanding of how costs are incurred is fundamental to a proper and efficient system of control. The research of the processes used can help us to complete our knowledge. This can then become the foundation of our accepted and future practices using sound knowledge as a basis rather than a series of rather general assumptions.

Techniques

If one examines the processes used by quantity surveyors 100 years ago and compares these with the methods in existence today we can see a dramatic change. Many of these changes are in the form of the techniques used, and would not have been developed but for the pioneer work of a few surveyors who were dissatisfied with old-fashioned procedures. The profession can never stand still, and increased knowledge can help us to develop new techniques for the future.

Cost advice

One of the quantity surveyor's roles in connection with any construction project is the provision of cost advice to clients and contractors. A proper understanding of the cost implications of construction will enable the quality of this cost advice to be improved. This is likely to place the quantity surveyor in greater demand, enhance his position and equip him for further roles in the future of the construction industry.

Results

Cost research in recent years has necessarily become more mathematical, often requiring the knowledge of algebraic and statistical methods and the possible applications of operational research. Using these methods has meant an understanding based upon empirical tests rather than a simple rule-of-thumb approach. This has allowed the natural use and development of the computer to be harnessed in the cost planning and cost control function. Research has also helped us to foresee the wider use of bills of quantities, simplified methods of calculating cost fluctuations, the way other countries assess building costs, how to reduce claims and the accuracy and reliability of building prices.

Describe the quantity surveyor's process of cost control in connection with a construction project.

Cost control embraces all methods of controlling the cost of construction projects within the limits of a determined sum, from inception of the scheme, throughout the design until final completion of the contract. The cost control of any construction project can be described under the following headings:

Preliminary estimate

This is the first indication of the cost of the proposed project, and is often the amount most remembered by the client. It should not, therefore, be too low as this may require some explanation as the design develops, should the cost increase; nor should it be too high as this may prohibit the design proceeding further due to the client's lack of funds. Drawings are unlikely to be available and only the vaguest information may be given.

Preliminary cost plans

These are prepared in order to evaluate the architect's first sketch designs. Sketch drawings of alternative designs may be available and the quantity surveyor will attempt to select the most economical or optimum solution. Optimum in this context may mean different solutions to different clients.

Cost plan

Once the architect has completed his final sketch design and this has been approved by the client, the formal cost plan should be produced. This will be developed from one of the preliminary cost plans and should now contain sufficient detail and description as a basis for the system of cost control. This can be a costly document to prepare and therefore it should not be embarked upon until the architect and the client are satisfied with the basic outline of the design.

Cost checks

As the design develops the architect will begin to produce working drawings. These should be checked to ensure that they reasonably comply with the anticipated design in respect of cost. The purpose of cost checking is to inform both the architect and the client of the effect of their design decisions on cost. The process does not seek to either stifle or dictate the design but hopes to avoid the possibilities of an abortive scheme. If at some later stage the design has to be revised because it exceeds the funds that are available, this can be both expensive and time-wasting. The aim of cost checking is to avoid this happening.

Bills of quantities stage

When the working drawings have been completed, these should be cost checked before bills of quantities are prepared. This will now become the main cost control document, particularly after it has been priced by a contractor. The quantity surveyor, in addition to carrying out his normal function of tender reporting, should also be able to reconcile the tender with his final cost plan. (The final cost plan is merely the cost plan that has been checked against the latest design.) If the process has been carried out properly, only minor modifications should need to be made to the overall cost of the scheme.

13

Post-contract cost control

It is sometimes wrongly assumed that the function of cost control ends with the receipt of tenders. In order to ensure that the control of cost is maintained, a process should be formulated until the final account is agreed. There are two methods used for post-contract cost control:

(1) Interim stage. The main process during this period is the preparation of interim valuations on the amount of work completed. This is in order that payment can be made to the contractor for the work carried out. In addition, the quantity surveyor should regularly inform the architect and client of the results of any changes in their design and the likely effect of these on the final account. These generally take the form of cost reports or financial statements.

(2) Final stage. The main process at this stage is to prepare and agree the final account for the project. Although some of this surveying work may have been undertaken during the preparation of interim certificates, the bulk of the work will now be finalised. Adjustments may have to be made to allow for:

(a) Provisional work.
(b) Variations approved by the architect.
(c) Daywork accounts.
(d) Adjustments for specialist suppliers and subcontractors accounts.
(e) Increased costs due to inflation.
(f) Compensation to the contractor on the basis of contractual claims.

In addition to these processes it is usual for the quantity surveyor to provide a cost analysis of the project based upon the tender sum. This may assist in providing the quantity surveyor with future cost information for other similar proposed projects.

3   Cost information

Describe the source and nature of cost information available to quantity surveyor.

The sources of cost data can be subdivided into the following groups, for easy reference.

Price books

The majority of price books are published annually, with the exception of the Cost Datafile which is published monthly. They are revised chiefly to take account of inflation, but there has been a gradual change in their layout, presentation and contents to meet current-day requirements. In periods of high inflation in the construction industry it is easy to see why this traditional price information soon becomes outdated. In practice, therefore, price books need to be updated by using indices or by some subjective assessment wherever possible.

Monthly cost data

There are several periodicals which now include cost information on materials prices and measured rates. Some include labour rates, indices, market indicators and other information relevant to construction costs. Although the rates included are current there is a serious disadvantage, due to limitations of space available, in that only the major items of work can be included. Research has shown that during periods of high inflation 35 per cent of all prices can change in a single month.

Only one source of cost information is available for works of civil engineering construction. This is perhaps due to the larger variation between prices for apparently the same item of work than might be expected on a typical building contract, and the differences in the method of estimating.

Building Cost Information Service

This is possibly the most extensive and comprehensive construction cost information service in the world. It provides a valuable service to its users on a reciprocal basis, whereby they in turn supply the service with actual cost data for redistribution amongst its members. It supplies extensive information on the cost analysis of completed projects and in addition provides cost indices, cost studies, cost trends, monthly briefings etc. In more recent years a separate service has been provided, aimed solely at the costs associated with the maintenance and repairs of building projects.

Priced bills of quantities

Priced bills of quantities provide a wealth of information for the quantity surveyor. It should be remembered, however, that the prices in bills are of a confidential nature and should not be disclosed to third parties without the contractor's permission. It is also important to remember the considerable variation in price that may occur between two apparently identical bill items. The cause of this variation is described as the vagaries of tendering and can be due to many different factors.

All the published information is based upon the compiler's view of what constitutes average prices for average projects carried out under average conditions. Where a quantity surveyor has maintained his own records he will be able to use them more easily and with greater confidence. It is also likely that this will reflect local conditions more accurately.

References

(1) 'Cost Index' published in *Building Specification* by Manning Rapley Publishing Limited, 42 High Street, Croydon, Surrey CR0 1YB, and prepared by consultant quantity surveyors.
(2) 'Cost File' published in *Building* by The Builder Limited, Builder House, PO Box 87, 1–3 Pemberton Row, Red Lion Course, Fleet Street, London EC4P 4HL and prepared by the Building Cost Information Service, 85–87 Clarence Street, Kingston-upon-Thames, Surrey.
(3) 'QS Datafile' published in *QS Weekly* by BWS Publishing Limited, 4 Addison Bridge Place, Kensington, London W14 9BR and compiled by Patrick Amos Chartered Surveyors.
(4) 'Estimating Supplement' published in *Building Trades Journal* by Northwood Publications, Elm House, 10–16 Elm Street, London WC1X 0BP and compiled by B. A. Waterfield, FCSI and E. H. King, BSc, MCSI.
(5) 'Measured Rates' published in *Civil Engineering* by Morgan-Grampian Construction Press Limited, 30 Calderwood Street, London SE18 6QH, and prepared by Davis Belfield and Everest, Chartered Quantity Surveyors.
(6) *Spons Architects and Builders Price Book* published by E. & F. Spon Limited, 11 New Fetter Lane, London EC4P 4EE, and edited by Davis Belfield and Evertest, Chartered Quantity Surveyors.
(7) *Laxtons Building Price Book 1980* published by Kelly's Directories Limited, Windsor Court, East Grinstead House, East Grinstead, West Sussex RH19 1XB and edited by N. R. Wheatlye, FRICS.
(8) *Griffiths Building Price Book* published by Baron Publishers, Newton Road, Yeovil, Somerset BA20 1NF and edited by G. H. Griffiths, FFS, FRSH.
(9) *Hutchins Priced Schedules* published by G. H. Lake & Co. Limited, 33 Station Road, Bexhill-on-Sea, Sussex and edited by G. Chrystal-Smith, AIAS, AIQS.
(10) *Cost Datafile* published by BWS Publishing Limited, 4 Addison Bridge Place, Kensington, London W14 9BR and compiled by Patrick Amos, DMS, ARICS, AIQS, MBIM.

(11) *Spons Mechanical and Electrical Services Price Book* published by E. & F. N. Spon Limited, 11 New Fetter Lane, London EC4P 4EE, and edited by Davis, Belfield and Everest, Chartered Quantity Surveyors.

(12) *Spons Landscape Price Book* published by E. & F. Spon Limited, 11 New Fetter Lane, London EC4P 4EE, and edited by Derek Lovejoy and Partners with pricing sections contributed by Gerald Horsefield and Partners and Widnell and Trollope, Chartered Quantity Surveyors.

(13) *The Schedule of Rates for Building Works* published by HMSO, Government Bookshops, 49 High Holborn, London WC1V 6HB and prepared by the Directorate of Quantity Surveying Development of the Property Services Agency.

(14) The Building Cost Information Service of the RICS, 85–87 Clarence Street, Kingston-upon-Thames, Surrey.

(15) The Building Maintenance Cost Information Service, 85–87 Clarence Street, Kingston-upon-Thames, Surrey.

Discuss the reliability of rates for measured works from bills of quantities.

Bills of quantities are a major source of cost information, but the information contained in them must be used with great care. Comparison of rates between two bills of quantities for the same project will show a considerable variation for many of the items. Although tenders may vary by only 10 per cent, individual trades may differ by as much as 40 per cent, and individual items by up to 200 per cent. Bills from different contractors for other projects can show variation in excess of these figures. When examining bill rates it is important that the surveyor has some idea of the rate expected, in order that a bill rate will not be used erroneously.

The surveyor in attempting to make use of rates from priced bills should not forget their confidentiality, and should not disclose their source to third parties (JCT clause 5.7).

Data from bills of quantities can be summarised as follows:

(1) Individual rates for measured items.
(2) Overall costs for use with the single price methods of approximate estimating, e.g. unit, square metre, cubic metre.
(3) Elemental format analysis.
(4) Basic price list of materials, if available.

The more detailed this information is presented, the more it will be subject to variability and hence the less towards reliability.

Computing average costs from a large number of projects has less relevance than examining costs from a few well-known projects. It is important when examining bills of quantities to understand the conditions that influenced the rates and prices charged.

Variations in rates may be due to any of the following factors:

(1) The size of the project.
(2) The type of project.
(3) The regional location of the project.
(4) The contract conditions applicable to the project.
(5) The market conditions prevalent at the time of tender for the project.
(6) The contract implications particularly affecting the contract period, and the account to be taken for inflation.

The following are further reasons for what has become known as the vagaries of tendering.

(1) Distribution of preliminary items. It is important to discover the extent to which preliminary items have been priced within this section, or alternatively allocated on a proportion basis amongst the measured items.

(2) Location of the site. The costs associated with projects in the countryside, or in the centres of busy towns and cities, vary and may reflect the problems of access, difficulties of performing the work etc.

(3) Deliberate distortion. The estimator may deliberately distort the bill rates either because he may be anticipating variations, or in order to obtain all the profit at an early stage in an attempt to finance the remainder of the work.

(4) Errors. It is not uncommon to find bill items priced incorrectly because of mistakes.

(5) Lack of accurate cost data. Owing to pressure of time, an estimator may be unable to price all the items analytically, and on some occasions this may be due to a lack of any available feedback on material prices.

(6) Facilities. A firm may be able to provide a more competitive price, for example where it has its own joiners' shop.

(7) Site techniques. The techniques that the contractor uses to complete the works (for example, the amount of mechanisation he uses) will be reflected in his prices.

(8) Sub-contractor's and supplier's prices. Contractors usually sub-let a proportion of their work to other contractors and suppliers.

(9) Standard of workmanship. Different standards of workmanship may be anticipated, depending upon the type of project, the standard of the specification and the requirements of the designer if known.

(10) Availability of labour. The availability of skilled labour is likely to vary at different times in the year and throughout the different regions of the country.

(11) Financial conditions. The financial ability of both the contractor and the client are likely to be reflected in the bill rates. For example, because of the shortage of work or the prestige of the project, the contract may have been 'bought'. It would be extremely unwise for the quantity surveyor to use such rates without caution.

(12) Special requirements. The examination of the contract documents may indicate some reasons for variability in prices, for example, an abnormal speed of construction, work required to be undertaken at unsocial hours, phasing etc.

The above is not a comprehensive list of items affecting the reliability of rates found in bills of quantities. Remember, too, that local conditions affecting the amount of work available, degree of competition etc. may not affect the overall national situation.

You are currently preparing a cost plan for a proposed warehouse on an urban centre site. You have available cost analyses for similar projects built in similar localities.

Analysis A contains preliminaries of £20 000 in a total of £200 000 and is dated August 1976.

Analysis B contains preliminaries of £54 000 in a total of £270 000 and is dated September 1975.

Analysis C contains preliminaries of £12 000 in a total of £240 000 and is dated May 1977.

Describe the use you may make of such data.

It is not uncommon, when examining priced bills of quantities, to find the preliminaries priced in different ways. The Building Cost Information Service standard form of cost analysis allows for showing the preliminaries as a separate element or for showing their costs apportioned amongst the other elements. Opinions differ as to whether preliminaries should be kept separate in an analysis, or spread in a proportionate value basis throughout the elements when reusing cost data.

Some contractors leave preliminaries apparently unpriced, whilst others include a lump sum which makes it impossible for the surveyor to understand the method of pricing. Sometimes at the last minute the contractor may have decided to revise his tender sum and adjust it by adding to or reducing the amount of preliminaries.

Preliminaries should be priced to reflect the varying site on-costs associated with the project e.g. temporary buildings, mechanical plant, scaffolding, temporary fencing, foreman in charge, distance to site etc. It should also include those costs that make the project peculiar or difficult to execute e.g. difficult labour areas, access and adjoining property or the short time scale for operations. The amount allocated for preliminaries may also reflect the type and nature of the project being constructed and the contractor's method of working e.g. use of tower cranes, hoists, prefabrication off site etc.

The value for preliminaries also depends to some extent on the tendering procedure and the type of contract envisaged. A negotiated contract, for example, is more likely to be priced in accordance with the expected procedures, than a contract that is priced independently. It is of particular importance, therefore, when examining and reusing cost information from bills of quantities, to be fully aware of all the circumstances relating to the project concerned.

The more the costs from a bill of quantities are examined in detail, the less reliable this data becomes. For example, the difference between the successful tenders for two apparently similar projects may be at the most 10 per cent, but the differences between identical bill items from these projects may be as high as 200 per cent.

Examination of the above three projects shows the preliminaries element distributed in the following way: Analysis A 10 per cent; Analysis B 20 per cent; Analysis C 5 per cent.

The large differences between the preliminaries in Analysis B and C are less likely to be caused by genuine contractual differences than by the pricing habits of the individual contractors. Where preliminaries are left unpriced, and their costs distributed among the individual bill rates, this can cause the bill rates to rise on average by about 10 per cent. Before any of the prices can be used it would be necessary to update them by use of indices to current prices.

Examination of the above three projects may suggest some exceptional project conditions in analysis B that are absent from the other two projects. Some of the preliminary costs from analysis C may be hidden within the bill rates, so distorting these rates or perhaps unbalancing the tender sum. Analysis, B, on the other hand, could have been a particularly unattractive project, and this has been shown by adding a lump sum amount to the preliminaries cost. It is unlikely that market conditions such as the amount of work available are a factor to consider, since the tender dates are so close together.

Similar items on each of the three projects are likely to have been priced differently because of the differences in the ways that the preliminaries have been priced. Examination of the updated rates may indicate this.

Assuming that there are no abnormal circumstances affecting any of the above three projects, apportioning the preliminaries cost to each of the elements provides the best basis for comparison before the data is reused. However, if the project has any abnormal features, it will be necessary to make additional separate allowances when estimating the costs.

If the preliminaries incorporated a sum for contingencies (an amount included and calculated at the architect's discretion), this should be eliminated before this adjustment is carried out.

It cannot be overemphasised that before a quantity surveyor attempts to reuse bill rates, he should have a detailed knowledge of the contractor and project concerned, and also an idea of the expected rate, in order to avoid using cost information erroneously.

Describe the adjustments that should be made to historic cost information when cost planning.

Although measured rates from priced bills of quantities or price books are frequently used during the cost planning process, the most useful data are contained in the cost analyses from previous projects. A cost analysis reveals the distribution of the cost of a building among its elements. The main factors which affect element costs are quantity, quality and price. In order to determine the effect of these factors on the cost of each individual element, the cost analysis must contain information on the specification of quality and quantity for each element, together with other data relating to the price level for the project as a whole. Three adjustments to the historic cost analysis are therefore necessary to account for quantity, quality and price. Occasionally, where the projects are almost identical, the qualitative and quantitive adjustments may be minimal. However, in our present economic climate, adjustments for price fluctuations nearly always have to be made.

(1) Adjustments for quantity. The quantity of an element is the actual amount of the element contained within the building. In a standard cost analysis it is described as the element unit quantity and is also sometimes referred to as the quantity factor. The cost of an element depends to a large extent upon quantity, therefore some measure of this needs to be provided in an analysis in order that adjustments can be made. Element unit quantities are expressed either in size (square metres) for elements such as walls, roof, floors, etc., or by number as in the case of sanitary fittings. Adjustments for quantity variations between two buildings require a simple arithmetical adjustment.

e.g.

Historic cost analysis

Element	Total cost	Cost per m² GIFA	Element unit quantity	Element rate
2 H. Internal doors	3734	0.31	$131\,m^2$	28.50

Proposed cost plan

The proposed project has 73 doors each size $1981 \times 762\,mm$. The element unit quantity is therefore $110\,m^2$. This is then multiplied by the element rate of £28.50 to give a total cost of £3135. This amount can then be divided by the proposed floor area of, say, $12\,000\,m^2$ to give a cost per m^2 gross internal floor area of £0.26.

(2) Adjustments for quality. The adjustment for differences in quantity described above is largely an objective exercise. Adjustments to allow for differences in quality are much more difficult to make and rely to some extent upon a personal interpretation between an historic analysis and the description of the proposed project. Where adjustments are necessary, they can be dealt with in the following ways:

(a) By using a separate analysis containing a similar specification. This can cause difficulties and inaccuracies because of the introduction of errors. (Errors from a single project tend to compensate each other.) In these circumstances it is preferable to make several analyses of the element in order to reduce any possible errors.

(b) By using approximate quantities for the revised specification. The danger can arise in that minor items can be omitted, resulting in a low estimate. All items must therefore be included, and an appropriate allowance added to cover these incidental items.

(3) Adjustments for price. The probable level of prices at the date of tender must be forecast and taken into account when preparing the cost plan. When the cost plan is prepared, prices in the historic cost analysis must then be converted to those forecast at the date of tender or, where prices are firm, tenders to allow for increases in prices during the contract period. Several construction cost and price indices are available to assist the quantity surveyor when updating or forecasting.

The following are some of the more important factors classified as price level adjustments: (a) Different tender dates. (b) Differences in contractors' prices relative to the general market price level. (c) Differences in site conditions, weather conditions etc. (d) Differences due to regional price variation.

The method of adjusting for price can either be on the basis of individual elements or as a single adjustment to the cost plan as a whole. Where data have been used from several cost analyses, the adjustment must be made on the basis of each element in turn.

Elemental cost analyses of projects are one of the most important sources of cost information available to the cost planner. Without them it would be difficult to set up a cost plan, and to test the viability of his estimates by comparison with other schemes. Standardisation in format and presentation is essential to enable them to be used for future data analyses. Standardisation is also important to facilitate comparisons between schemes.

4 Approximate estimating

There are several methods that can be used for the preparation of cost plans and approximate estimates. Summarise these methods, stating the degree of reliability of each method.

Unit method

This method is based upon the cost per place, and is based upon the fact that a close relationship exists between the cost of a building and the number of functional units it accommodates. Historic cost data is collected from previously completed similar projects in the form of total costs and the number of places. The method is very accurate when applied to projects such as schools, where the method is often used to set a cost limit.

Cube method

This is the traditional method and is now rarely used in practice. The costs per cubic metre from completed projects are used to calculate the costs of future projects. Because of the large scale of figures involved, significant inaccuracies can occur.

Superficial area method

The costs per square metre of gross internal floor area are readily available and easily calculated from completed projects. This is a popular method because it relates cost to an easily-understood quantity. Accuracy is sometimes claimed to be within ±5 per cent, although luck plays some part in the assessment. With this method, the available rates need to be subjectively adjusted to take account of prevailing market conditions etc. It is often used when a very early estimate is required and the approximate floor area is the only data available.

Storey enclosure method

This method, although relatively new, has been quickly superseded by other methods. It is based upon an amalgamation of the areas for walls, floors and roofs. Historic data are difficult to obtain. It is claimed to be a more accurate method of approximate estimating than by using the single-quantity methods.

Approximate quantities

The project is measured very broadly and rates are applied to their all-in quantities. The accuracy of the estimate should be improved over previous methods. The estimate, however, takes longer to prepare and more information is needed.

Parametric cost analysis

This method uses a combination of gross internal floor area and the building's perimeter. Rates are not available unless calculated by individual surveyor. It is claimed that accuracy is better than that obtained from using the gross internal floor area alone.

Cost planning

These methods use approximate estimating techniques coupled with cost analysis data. They are the only techniques that can be used to check the costs of the design as it develops. They should ensure that the tender sum comes within the forecasted cost. Because of the time and cost involved, they have not become the standard practice that might have been expected. Two forms of cost planning are:
(a) *Elemental*, where the scheme is costed to fit within an overall cost limit.
(b) *Comparative*, where the scheme is costed in a variety of ways to select the optimum solution.

Cost models

These are a new generation method of forecasting and determining the cost of proposed projects. They are statistical methods and can only really be attempted if computer-assisted. It is claimed that accuracy is improved, particularly at inception stage. They are still very much in development.

Generally, the easier the method of measuring, the more difficult, and hence the more inaccurate, will be the pricing. Unless rates are easily obtainable and currently available the method suggested will find little acceptance in practice. Research is constantly being undertaken to improve the accuracy and reliability of the costs of proposed construction projects.

Describe the construction of a cost model, and indicate its advantages and disadvantages over the traditional methods that may be used in practice.

Cost modelling is a technique that can be used to forecast the estimated cost of a proposed construction project. Although it has been heavily researched in the academic world there is only scant evidence of it ever being used in professional practice. The circumstances when it could be usefully applied in practice are:

(1) At the initial stage of a construction project, it has been shown to be a viable alternative to other methods available on certain types of civil engineering projects.
(2) In place of approximate estimating and cost planning. The existing methods available are relatively new, and resistance to change is therefore not as entrenched.

(3) In preference to analytical methods for estimating by contractors. Estimators are fairly conservative in their approach, so for cost modelling to replace the traditional methods it would have to give consistently more accurate results.

Construction of a cost model

The following are the usual stages in the development of a cost model.

(1) Defining the type of model to be constructed. This may be a single model for the entire project, or individual models representing a trade, an element, an operation etc.

(2) Collection of suitable data. Every form of estimating relies heavily upon some type of suitable historic data. Before cost modelling can begin, sufficient accurate and reliable data, suitable for predictive purposes, are needed. A minimum amount of data is always required to make the model statistically reliable. The type of data collected will depend upon the type of model being constructed.

(3) Selection of an appropriate technique. Several different methods can be used for cost modelling purposes. A popular and applicable technique used is that of multiple linear regression analysis. This is a statistical technique to find a formula or mathematical model that best describes the data available. The technique is used in those situations where the relationship between the variables is not unique. A model could be constructed to predict, for example, either cost or price. Other techniques used include that of simulation.

(4) Computer applications. The arithmetic involved in multiple linear regression analysis is considerable and the practical application can only be undertaken by the use of a computer. Appropriate software can usually be obtained and access to the computer should then be a very straightforward process.

(5) Analysis of model. Once the 'best' model has been constructed, it needs to undergo statistical testing.

(6) Testing the model. The final model would then be tested using new data, and any deterioration measured. Some deterioration would be expected to account for new variability in the fresh data. Other tests could be carried out to compare the model predictability against the actual values obtained from further projects.

(7) Model in use. When a successful model has been developed and applied in practice, it can be continually refined to adapt to any changing patterns or trends.

The advantages and disadvantages of cost modelling can be summarised as follows.

Advantages

(1) Cost information can be provided more quickly, and changes in the building's design can be easily cost-updated.

(2) More information is generated from the use of the computer, so that more informed decisions can be made.

(3) The information should be more reliable, introducing greater confidence into the decision-making process.
(4) Comparable cost information for the designer can be produced earlier in the design process with the same degree of reliability.

Disadvantages

(1) Cost modelling requires the use of new knowledge.
(2) Because the approach is so radical, there will be some resistance to change and its use in practice.
(3) An appropriate computer, together with the necessary software, is necessary.

Outline the problems encountered in the preparation of preliminary estimates, and suggest ways in which present techniques can be improved.

Preliminary estimates are generally prepared on the basis of scant information, about both the particular project concerned and also the amount of suitable cost information. Estimating the cost of a future project consists of two processes: measurement and pricing. It can be reasonably argued that the easier the method of measuring, the more difficult it will be to arrive at a reliable and accurate price.

The techniques used today vary from the unit method to the superficial floor area and approximate quantities. Other methods, such as the cube rules and storey enclosure method, are largely for the history books. Cost planning is not normally introduced at this stage of the design process. More elaborate methods such as parametric cost analysis and, more specifically, cost modelling have not been used with any enthusiasm or expertise, although the latter method has been used successfully for major roadworks projects.

The problems of preparing a preliminary estimate are, therefore, twofold:

Measurement

Here, the quantity surveyor needs to obtain suitable quantifiable data from the client's information or brief. The information available may consist of nothing more than the building type, size and number of storeys. Details about the specification level to be applied and the quality and quantity of services and fittings can often only be determined from similar previous projects, or the quantity surveyor's own knowledge and experience. Even where the information is available, in the form of a drawing, this is likely to be in outline form only.

Pricing

The quantity surveyor, when providing a client with a preliminary estimate, has to predict not the 'going' price for the project, but the price at which a contractor is prepared to carry out the work. In making this prediction, the quantity surveyor will objectively view past recorded data for similar work and will update and amend this to account for inflation, regional variation, shape, height, etc. He will also subjectively revise his calculated estimate to allow for market conditions and the price in relationship to other known current tenders received, using his intuition.

Contractors themselves cannot estimate without error. Indeed an estimate will, by definition, be inaccurate. The degree of accuracy (proved by research) is much worse than contractors believe and is in the order of ± 10 per cent on average. This means that while some estimates will be near to their true costs, others will be wildly inaccurate. It can also be shown that contractors who make the largest negative errors often win the contract.

The quantity surveyor, therefore, when preparing his preliminary estimate has not only to take into account the appropriate rates for the measured works, and to make some allowance for regional and local variation and market conditions; but he must also be aware that the contractor's tender sum will in itself be 'a moving target'. The quantity surveyor must 'allow' for the contractor's inaccuracies, and try to predict his future tender sum. It is not surprising, therefore, that the quantity surveyor's degree of accuracy is on average about ± 13 per cent. This figure is supported by current research projects and results.

In order to improve the reliability of preliminary estimates, here are four suggestions:

(1) Improve the quality and type of preliminary design data supplied by the architect and client to the quantity surveyor.
(2) Consider better ways of quantifying the data available at the design stage, and correlating this with cost.
(3) Examine the methods by which the contractor may produce more accurate estimates. This may require a completely new approach to estimating techniques. It might require the examination of operational estimating, cost modelling and computerised systems.
(4) Enhance the quality of cost information available to the quantity surveyor. He currently has available priced bills, price books, estimating data and access to the Building Cost Information Service. More data may be required than can be quickly analysed from either a central or a local storage system by a computer.

You have been asked to produce a budget estimate for a proposed scheme to convert a dilapidated three-storey riverside Victorian warehouse into offices (with showrooms) for an owner-occupier. No drawings or specification have yet been produced.

Describe how you would proceed, discuss the most important factors you would need to take into account before reporting a figure, and state any qualifications you would consider it necessary to make.

First, the quantity surveyor should visit the site to examine the condition of the building. It is also important for him to have some idea of the type of client involved with the development, as this may influence the project. For example, an over-ambitious client may feel that the premises could be satisfactorily converted for any type of use; and this may not be true. In some circumstances it may be economically more sensible to demolish and completely redevelop. So it must be established that the building can be economically converted and that some form of structural survey has already demonstrated this. It must also be remembered that the refurbishment of buildings can cost up to 75 per cent of the new cost, excluding any demolition. It is assumed that the planning authorities are not objecting to a change of use of the premises.

During his site visit, the quantity surveyor needs to examine particularly those parts of the building that are in need of repair and are therefore a cost element in his estimate. Furthermore, he should have some knowledge of construction methods employed during the Victorian period. In examining the condition of the building he needs to satisfy himself on the following points:

(1) The suitability of the existing foundations for the type of conversion considered. The existing building was used as a warehouse, and its proposed use is for offices and showrooms. This should not present any structural problems, although any signs of settlement should be looked for, that might occur with an old riverside building.
(2) A damp-proof course is unlikely to have been incorporated in the original building, and added to this the building is standing on a river bank. Some allowance in the estimate therefore needs to be made towards elimination, treatment and prevention of dampness. If the warehouse included a basement, this could be a particularly troublesome area in this respect.
(3) Any building decay due to insect, vermin or fungus attack should be noted. If such decay is found it may be prudent to invite a specialist contractor to visit the site to provide an indication of its extent and an approximate cost for its eradication.
(4) The overall condition of the existing structure, including: the external walls which will need repointing and cleaning, other loadbearing walls, the floor construction and the roof.
(5) The general condition or impression of the building and its suitability for refurbishment. It should be noted that the building is in a dilapidated condition, which indicates some considerable remedial work in the above areas.

Accepting that its condition is appropriate for conversion, the quantity surveyor then needs to assess the possible work to be undertaken. He needs at least some verbal guidance on the intentions of the client, and should consider the following:

(1) The structural work necessary. Some demolition and alteration work will be envisaged. This might include demolishing walls, forming or building up openings, the possible replacement of the existing (timber?) floors and the removal of unwanted items such as fittings and other debris. Some new structural work will also be required in the remodelling process.
(2) The standard of finishings required throughout. This may vary between the offices and the showroom and some indication of these locations is required. Suspended ceilings, for example, would probably be a necessity throughout.
(3) Completely new engineering services must be allowed for in the estimate, and some indication of their extent and type is needed for plumbing, heating, air conditioning, electrical and protective installations such as fire fighting and security.
(4) New stairways in new positions, and the possibility of installing a lift. Certainly if the showroom extended beyond the ground floor, a lift would become a necessity.
(5) New windows and doors will be required and it is important to know the client's requirements regarding furniture or fittings to be provided under the contract.
(6) External works, which may require the construction of a new car park and, for prestige or planning purposes, some landscaping.

The best approach to produce a budget estimate might be on the basis of approximate quantities, where the proposed work could be measured very broadly and a description of the quality envisaged could be given. Any assumptions on the standard of the existing warehouse, together with the proposals outlined above, would also be described. It would also be useful to give some indication on market conditions, the best method of obtaining a contractor and a likely start and completion date envisaged. The information would probably be best presented in the style of a report.

In a period of general economic recession you are accused of professional negligence because your estimate for conversion of an old warehouse of 200 m² gross floor area into low-rent craft workshops is £5000 above the lowest tender. Reply to your client's accusation.

It is difficult with questions of this type to assess such an estimate without knowing more details. Based upon the information we have available, viz old warehouses' conversion, low-rent workshops, £40 000 might be the figure involved (200 m² × £200). Possibly a minimum amount of work is envisaged to bring it up to some sort of standard for a workshop. Walls may be removed, some structural work is possible, any defects will be rectified, but the quality of the finishings is likely to be of a low standard and the amount of modernisation work may be minimal. It is, however, necessary to have some idea of an approximate estimate in order to understand the magnitude of the error. It is worth mentioning here that a RICS study showed that the average estimating accuracy by quantity surveyors was in the order of 13 per cent.

Had the quantity surveyor's estimate been below the lowest tender sum, some complaint might have been expected. A quantity surveyor hopes that his estimate is comparable with the lowest tender, and in most circumstances hopes to be in second place immediately above this figure. The estimate is, in any case, only an indication of an expected tender sum. If our project did cost £40 000 then the quantity surveyor's error is 12½ per cent and this fits in well with the figure suggested above. Moreover, the percentage error would be expected to be substantially greater on a small project, such as this, than on a larger one.

In a general economic recession, tender sums can become very unpredictable, with some contractors pricing jobs only at cost in order to stay in business. As a recession deepens, tender prices actually fall, and projects that may in normal times have proved unattractive are awarded to contractors at very acceptable prices, as far as the clients are concerned. In circumstances like this, the period of time between the preparation of the approximate estimate and the actual tenders will be very important and could have a significant influence on any discrepancy that might occur between the approximate estimate and the contractor's tender.

Small-scale alteration projects are very difficult to estimate by either the quantity surveyor or the contractor. It must also be remembered that the contractor's price, whilst being a sum for the work to be carried out, is in itself subject to some degree of error. The quantity surveyor may have prepared his approximate estimate on the basis of measured quantities, and at that time drawings and other information may have been very scant. Although any changes in his assumptions on cost are given to the architect, the amounts involved are not usually significant.

The quantity surveyor holds himself as being qualified to do the work entrusted to him. If he does not have the level of skill or experience which is usual in the profession, or if he does not use his skills to the full, he will be guilty of negligence. In order for the workshop owner to succeed in an action for negligence, he will have to prove the following:

(1) That the quantity surveyor owed him a duty of care. Clearly, if the quantity surveyor is being paid for his services, this point would be established.
(2) That the quantity surveyor's error was carelessly made, and he did not perform his duty in a reasonable manner. Can the difference between the estimate and the tender be shown to be of such a magnitude (because that is the argument) that it was carelessly calculated? Clearly not, if we examine published data on the accuracy of estimating. Did he perform the work in a reasonable manner? If it could be shown that, under the same circumstances, other quantity surveyors would have been able to provide a more accurate estimate than was given to the client, it could then be argued that he did not perform his duty in a reasonable manner. If this was not so, no case for negligence could be considered.

(3) That the workshop owner suffered damage. Had the estimate been too low, it could have been argued (but probably unsuccessfully) that the client had been misled, was unable to afford his building and was responsible for fees and no building to show for it.

At the tender stage some amendments could be made to the design in order to expend the apparent £5000 saving. This would seem to be the reasonable course of action under these circumstances, if this was the client's wish.

It must not be forgotten, however, that the surveyor is responsible for his estimate, and it must be reasonably accurate to have any value. If a surveyor delivers an estimate that is widely at variance with the tender sum, then as well as being possibly guilty of negligence, he is also failing to provide a reasonable service.

What are the problems associated with the pricing of preliminary items? Describe the items that a quantity surveyor should consider when attempting to provide cost information for a client.

Design teams need to attempt to estimate real costs. This presents greater difficulties in the construction industry than almost any other industry. The reasons for this are twofold. First, and most important, there are the difficulties arising from the separation of design from construction; and secondly, design staff have only limited knowledge about building costs. These two factors affect the reliability and accuracy of all building costs and none more so than preliminaries. Given that the prevailing situation – design by one party and construction by another – is unlikely to change in the near future, the problems of estimating this work by the design staff can be summarised as follows.

(1) The preliminaries element is more directly influenced by the choice of the construction method than is any other section. The method is generally unknown at the time of design cost planning, and the real costs that should be attributable cannot therefore be accurately forecast. Accepting that in circumstances where the design and construction method is defined, and inaccuracy in estimating still occurs, the assessment of preliminary costs can be little better than a 'guess' at the design stage.
(2) The examination of several cost analyses from previous projects will illustrate how variably this section can be priced. The percentage of the cost attributable to preliminary items can vary considerably between different projects, and for no apparent reason. Where one is able to examine priced bills of quantities for the same project, the differences in costs between identical items can be considerable and do not reflect realistic price differences.
(3) Preliminaries are often used at tendering stage to make last-minute adjustments which do not reflect or represent the true costs of this section of the works and so make their analysis difficult in practice.

Preliminaries at the design stage are often calculated as a percentage of the total of the remainder of the work. The percentage is usually assessed on the basis of previous projects, an inspection of the analyses being used and the interpretation of the available drawings. The following items may considerably affect the percentage allowed for the preliminaries element.

(1) Location. This includes entry to and egress from the site, the distance from major roads and the requirements regarding the provision of temporary roads on site. It would also include any requirements regarding costs of travelling and subsistence payments for operatives and staff.

(2) Space on site. Limited space on site for the storage of materials and the facilities required for office and canteen accommodation may result in working in confined areas or the occupation on site of existing buildings prior to demolition.

(3) Security. The need for temporary fencing, hoardings and gantries for the safety of the public, and the requirements for protection from vandalism and pilfering, often have to be considered.

(4) Contract period. Many of the items included within this section are assessed on the basis of a time analysis in conjunction with the value of the project. A short contract period may necessitate overtime and weekend working. Whether or not the project will be awarded with increased costs will also be an important consideration.

(5) Contingencies. Although these are not strictly preliminary items the quantity surveyor will often attempt to include them in his estimate or cost plan at the same time as he assesses the preliminary costs.

(6) Plant. Some items of plant that can be directly related to the measured works are included with that work section. Other items of plant that may be required for several trades are more conveniently priced in preliminaries. Items such as scaffolding, hoists and tower cranes come within this latter grouping.

(7) Insurance. During the assessment of the preliminary items it is useful to attempt to determine insurance costs, noting the provisions of the conditions.

The assessment of the preliminaries element is influenced most by the type of construction and the size of the building. However, each is composed of a different set of requirements giving each preliminary element a special nature. The construction programme, total size, area, building height, shape and the closeness of adjacent buildings are other factors to consider.

5 Cost planning

Suggest how the cost planning process might be affected because of the more extensive use of computers by quantity surveyors.

Quantity surveyors first attempted to use the computer in the early 1960s for producing bills of quantities. This was a natural choice and application since it was, and still is, the main function of the majority of quantity surveying practices, and also because it was a suitable type of work for data processing. There were, in those early days, many disadvantages of using computers, and operating costs were such that many quantity surveying practices were unable to justify their use on that basis alone. However, with the advent of less expensive computer power in the form of minicomputers and microprocessors, many quantity surveyors now harness them for a variety of functions. They are currently used in, for example, fees calculations, salaries analysis, office job costings and word processing. In addition they are used for estimating, valuations, NEDO formula and cost planning.

The use of computers for cost planning purposes is still in its infancy. Indeed the entire process of cost planning, as we know it in theory and practice today, is little over 20 years old. In order to make the current process of cost planning more efficient, it is worth considering introducing computers in the following areas.

Cost data

The first aspect to consider in cost planning is the provision of an adequate cost data base. The poor quality and content of available cost information today is often criticised. One of the reasons why the data produced are inconsistent and unreliable is that they have been assembled on too narrow a base.

A sufficient quantity and quality of data has not been available, and even if it were, the present manual processes would be unable to cope with it. It is therefore envisaged that a central construction cost data bank will be formulated, on the basis of computerised storage and retrieval. Surveyors may, in addition, wish to retain and store their own data on their own personal computers, but this on its own is likely to prove inadequate for the wider and more precise nature of future cost planning.

Construction cost data will be supplied to this central store on a reciprocal basis in much the same way that the BCIS currently operates. One of the major differences, however, will be the way in which this information is assessed. Currently the bulk of this information passing to and fro in the profession is on a postal basis. Any future system is likely to be a computerised one linked by an appropriate Post Office network.

Cost planning process

Any future cost planning development can only take place by using the computer. A manual method, however sophisticated, will be inadequate for the following reasons.

Flexibility – it must be capable of measuring and pricing construction work at the different levels of design. It must provide for a range of estimating techniques.

Accuracy – current levels of accuracy in this process are unacceptable. It has been shown that the only way to improve this is by way of providing more extensive data.

Ease and speed of application.

Ease of maintenance – the system must be capable of regular updating in order to provide the current information.

It is unlikely also that more information than what is currently considered standard or adequate will be needed. Cost advice on alternative initial design solutions will need to be coupled with many other factors such as life cycle costing, financial and taxation implications, grants and allowances. Only with the help and speed of computer power is it possible to provide immediate answers to these questions, asked by influential clients.

Communication aspects

The communications industry support initially grew out of the recognition that exchanging data between computers would become a necessity. On a simplified basis we are already able, via our television screens and the Prestel and Viewdata networks, to gain access to considerable information. This will probably be considered negligible when compared with the information available in a few years time. Some mechanisation is already present in today's quantity surveyors' offices. In the future there will be even greater mechanisation, where the quantity surveyor will have, in addition to much of the commonplace equipment of today, links to some national computer network. He will also have facilities capable of recording drawn information (known as facsimile transmission) with coupled photocopying machines for producing hard copies.

You have prepared a detailed estimate and cost plan for a 20-storey office block. The client is, however, considering varying his original requirements and as a result you will shortly be asked to estimate the financial effect of these modifications. Describe the factors you would consider when making an estimate for the following variations: (1) addition of a further five storeys; (2) addition of air conditioning; (3) omission of a basement car park; (4) substitution of ordinary glazing by solar reflective glazing in the curtain walling; (5) upgrading the office block from a speculative building intended for sale to an owner-occupied prestige building.

(1)(a) The use of alternative and more expensive foundations made necessary because of the increased loading from the taller building. The type of foundations contemplated for the 20-storey block may prove to be adequate depending upon the ground condition. An overall reduction in the cost per square metre of the gross internal floor area would be expected for this element.

(b) An increase in the structural strength of the frame would be required to accommodate the extra loads, and this would result in an increase in the overall cost of the scheme.

(c) Although the 20-storey building would be designed with wind loading in mind, a 25 per cent increase in height could result in a more expensive redesign to account for this factor.

(d) The increased costs associated with building at heights, including vertical transportation, reduced outputs and compliance with the appropriate wage allowances laid down by the National Working Rule Agreement.

(e) Additional costs associated with engineering services in respect of larger supply and discharge pipes and the increased capacity of pumps.

(f) An increase in the number of lifts required, because of the additional floors to be served, together with an increase in the cost of the remaining lifts (the recommendation (average) is one lift per four floors depending upon the occupation factors).

(g) The extra costs associated with the increased occupancy, e.g. circulation areas, car parking facilities.

(h) A longer contract period required because of the larger project and its associated increase in cost.

(2)(a) The costs of the air-conditioning plant and equipment including ducts, fans and air-treatment equipment and controls.

(b) The costs of associated builders' work in connection with this element.

(c) The costs of providing available space and a housing for the air-conditioning plant.

(d) The costs of improved sound insulation that may be needed to reduce any noise from the air-conditioning system.

(e) The provision of space, possibly above the suspended ceiling, to accommodate the air-conditioning ducts, resulting in increased storey height.

(f) Some adjustment to the originally-anticipated heating system in order to achieve compatibility with the air-conditioning system.

35

(3)(a) The costs associated with any alternative car parking facility.

(b) The alternative costs of appropriate foundations.

(c) If the basement were to be used for storage or to accommodate plant and equipment, alternative space would be needed.

(d) The costs of an access road to the basement would be saved.

(4)(a) Solar reflective glazing will keep the building cooler inside during the summer.

(b) The increased costs of the solar reflective glazing.

(c) A possible saving in window blinds.

(d) A reduction in the efficiency of the ventilation due to reduced air currents, and the costs associated with improved ventilation.

(5)(a) An improvement in the overall standard of finishings, both internally and externally, e.g. floor coverings, external facing materials, suspended ceilings, etc.

(b) The provision of high-quality maintenance-free construction, e.g. aluminimum windows.

(c) An improved space layout, including the use of high-quality construction for internal partitions.

(d) An improvement in the quality of engineering services, particularly items such as plumbing appliances, lighting equipment, etc.

(e) The fitting-out costs of a speculative building are often provided by the eventual owner. A prestige owner-occupied building is more likely to include these items within the contract sum.

(f) Some type of landscaping may be required for the prestige office building.

(g) The costs associated with the provision of a foyer.

(h) Consideration of using a different building contractor in order to provide a higher standard of workmanship.

Describe how you would modify a cost plan to take account of each of the following events (assuming that no provision had already been made for them).

(1) 15 per cent increase in labour rates to take effect three months after commencement of contract.
(2) Substantial increase in rates of interest on borrowed money three months prior to tender date.
(3) Sharp reduction in public spending on building works six months prior to commencement of contract.
(4) 14 per cent currency devaluation three months prior to tender date.

(1) This is a common situation for surveyors to deal with and currently arises annually when the building operatives are awarded a pay increase. If the contract were to be placed on a fully fluctuating basis, and the cost plan were to be calculated to forecast the tender sum, then no adjustment would be required. If, however, the contract were to be awarded on either a fixed-price basis or it was necessary to predict the final account sum, the following adjustment would need to be made.

It would first be necessary to analyse the proposed project between labour, materials and plant costs. This might show for example:

Labour 55 per cent
Materials 40 per cent
Plant 5 per cent

In this adjustment to the cost plan there is no alteration needed to the costs of materials or plant.

Secondly, it is necessary to know the likely duration of the proposed project. The additional sum to be allowed in the cost plan for the increases in labour rates would be as follows:

Allowance for increase in labour rates = increase in labour rates × labour content in proposed project × amount of cost plan × contract duration (less three months) ÷ contract duration.

The allowance could then be apportioned amongst the elements. It might be argued that to reduce the contract duration by three months is unrealistic, since the labour allocation to a project is smaller at the start of a project than when the project is in full production. The alternative approach is to try to determine the actual labour proportion expected during these three months or, because it is minor compared with the whole, to ignore it.

(2) An increase in interest rates can have two effects. First, because the majority of contractors operate on the basis of using some borrowed money, their overall costs will increase. This increase might have to be recovered from future construction projects, and therefore the cost of the proposed scheme will increase. It may be necessary, therefore, to determine a contractor's typical borrowing requirements and then to calculate the approximate extra costs associated with the rise in interest charges. It might already be assumed that the contractor has taken steps to ensure prompt payment, thereby reducing any costs associated with delayed payments. The

increase in the rate of interest charged will also have the effect of increasing the costs and charges of manufacturers and suppliers from whom the contractor purchases his materials.

The second effect of an increase in interest rates may be to cause some proposed projects to be shelved. Interest rates will also affect clients and developers and can make previously viable schemes uneconomic. This will reduce the amount of future work available and thereby increase the scope for competition. Contractors will then either have to improve their own productivity, be prepared to accept smaller returns or curtail some of their activities.

(3) The public sector is a large client of the construction industry. Any reduction in the overall level of the public sector's building programme will have an adverse effect on the construction industry. Contractors currently heavily involved in public sector building will try to seek alternative sources of work in the private sector. This will have the effect of increasing competition and so reduce prices. If prices are at a particularly low level (as in 1982) then it is difficult to see how contractors could realistically lower them any further without taking exceptional risks.

(4) This currency devaluation will have the effect of increasing the costs of future imported raw materials and manufactured goods. It would be necessary for the quantity surveyor to evaluate the costs of such items already included in his cost plan and increase their value by the appropriate amount. Alternatively he may be able to suggest UK alternatives that although were previously more expensive are now shown to be more cost-effective. If there is already a fixed limit to the cost plan, less expensive methods of construction may need to be examined in order for the cost plan to remain the same.

The currency devaluation may have the spin-off effect of increased demand for home-produced goods, that in the long term could necessitate new factories and warehousing and associated work.

The professional approach to cost control requires a constant monitoring of factors influencing prices. Identifying these influences and measuring their effects on proposed building costs is necessary in order to update cost plans.

An architect has prepared several outline plans for a client's proposed new building project. Although they all offer a similar amount of accommodation, the designs vary considerably. What advice could you provide for the client to help him select the most appropriate solution?

The quantity surveyor is often called upon to provide economic comparisons of alternative design solutions. The costs of building design solutions are influenced by many factors, some of which are interrelated. When making these comparisons, it is useful to the design team to express costs in terms of user requirements, such as the costs per square metre of gross internal floor area.

The following are the main factors to be considered in any assessment between competing design proposals. The location of the site and ground conditions are not considered because they will be common to all schemes. The grouping of buildings, although not envisaged as an alternative here, is of cost signficance but is being considered elsewhere.

The examination of the following factors do not seek to restrict or limit the architect and his design. Their aim is to inform the client on the economic consequences of various designs and to help him to select the most appropriate design solution.

Planning efficiency

Although each outline plan is similar in overall floor area, the way that this area is allocated within the project will be of particular importance to the client. The architect will have attempted to have made the best possible use of space within each design, but the ratio between usable and non-usable areas (circulation space) will differ.

An economic layout will have, as one of its main aims, the reduction of circulation space to a minimum. The ratio of non-usable floor area will be dependent upon the building's function, but in the cause of planning efficiency this should not exceed 20 per cent. The elimination of lengths of corridor resulting in communication through other rooms, or 'open-plan' design, may not be acceptable, whilst reducing the widths of corridors may not be permissable under regulations. On the other hand, the client of a prestige block of offices or flats may require large entrance and foyer areas to provide images of grandeur, and this will obviously reduce the planning efficiency.

Plan shape

The plan shape of any building greatly affects costs. The more complex the shape of the building, the higher will be its cost per square metre of gross internal floor area. The additional costs will not be solely attributable to the larger area of external walls, but other elements also will be affected, and there will be increased costs directly as a result of the work being more complicated. A square shape in the majority of cases provides the most economic solution. The client, however, will need to balance this factor with the need for planning efficiency and the desire for external aesthetics. Moreover, the simplest plan shape is not always the most economic proposition. For example, for buildings on sloping sites involving large amounts of cut and fill, a rectangular shape running with the contours may be more appropriate. Also, for buildings requiring natural day-lighting to all parts, or structures that will have heavy floor loadings, the square shape might not be the most suitable form.

Height

The constructional costs of tall buildings is greater than low-rise structures offering the same units of accommodation. Tall buildings are generally only preferred where land is either expensive or in scarce supply. High-rise buildings generally necessitate expensive foundations, structural frames, lifts, expensive fire regulations and improved engineering services and these are some of the reasons for the greater costs of construction.

The storey height of buildings is largely determined by the needs of the user of the building. Differing storey heights may have been selected depending upon the necessity to accommodate the appropriate engineering services within a false ceiling space. The storey height directly affects the costs of external walls and partitions, together with their necessary finishings and decorations. It may also indirectly affect the provision and running costs of engineering services and the vertical circulation elements.

Constructional details

In order for the quantity surveyor to advise the client on the implications of the constructional methods proposed, cost studies of the more important elements are made. These can be expensive in surveyor's time, and only those elements which are cost-sensitive are analysed in detail. Cost studies are not normally undertaken in circumstances where the cost difference between alternatives is obviously going to make very little change to the overall costs. Where a cost study reveals only a marginal saving, it would be inappropriate for the quantity surveyor to lay great emphasis upon such a result. In connection with new processes or technologies, the surveyor should remember that contractors are likely to be rather wary and price the work accordingly.

The constructional details can have an important influence upon the contract period required. The use of standard or prefabricated components will shorten this period and will be a factor to be considered by the client in this respect.

Costs in use

When the construction work is complete and the building is being used, costs-in-use will depend upon the type of client. All types of building allow for energy saving, either by design or through the building regulations. The emphasis of providing improved thermal insulation does, however, still depend upon whether the project is for owner occupation, sale or lease. The disadvantages and disruptions caused by repairs and maintenance should be balanced with the need for future modernisation and improvement. It should also be remembered that providing the most expensive type of construction initially does not always result in cost savings in the future.

Discuss the importance of cost checking during the cost planning process.

Once a satisfactory cost plan has been accepted by the architect, cost checking can start on the more detailed design. The cost plan is a statement of the proposed expenditure divided between the elements of the building. Each elemental cost is regarded as a cost target and the process of cost checking involves comparing these amounts with the architect's developing design, and reporting on any differences. Where a system of cost limits applies this may mean either redistributing funds from other elements, using money that may possibly be held in reserve, or redesigning that element to fit within the agreed total cost. It is important to carry out these cost checks as soon as possible after the development of the design. This will thus avoid too much abortive work on the part of the architect should the design prove too costly. Difficulties at tender stage necessitating some pruning of the scheme and the preparation of an addendum bill of quantities should then be a problem of the past.

The advantages to the client of cost checking the design are that he can be fully aware of the cost implications of all design decisions, and that he will have reasonable assurance that his budget estimate will not be exceeded. He will also be able to avoid the frustrations in time and expense of seeing his design revised.

Cost checking is a time-consuming process, particularly if major discrepancies occur between the quantity surveyor's cost plan and the architect's design. Time can be saved if the surveyor has provided the architect with a detailed cost plan with specification descriptions, and where the architect has not diverged too far from these assumptions. If the cost plan was based upon a previous similar project for the same architect and client, the cost-checking process will be a negligible part of the surveyor's work. If, however, the project under examination is strictly a one-off design with no similar project with which to compare, then great care must be taken with the cost checking in order to achieve the desired results.

Once the working drawings are available, the quantity surveyor's main role will be the taking-off of quantities for the preparation of the bill of quantities. It is usually a hectic time in the office with very little spare time for other duties. If the cost checking is to be effective, this should be done prior to taking-off and the surveyor should resist the temptation to put it off until later. This could mean, should this part of the design be too elaborate, a few rubbings-out on the part of the architect, but a completely wasted take-off on the part of the quantity surveyor.

The amount of time and care spent by the surveyor depends to a large extent on the importance of the element. Those elements that are cost-sensitive need the greatest attention, but minor elements cannot simply be ignored.

The pricing of the cost checks will be undertaken in a similar manner to the original cost plan. The quantity surveyor must be vigilant in the use of rates from the various sources, but more so from bills of quantities where some rates can be misleading. Perhaps during the later stages of cost checking, detailed and firm quotations for the specialist works will have been received which can now be substituted for the previously approximate amounts.

If the process of cost checking has been carried out thoroughly, then the receipt of tenders should provide few surprises. It is nevertheless useful to carry out some form of cost reconciliation to highlight any discrepancies between the final cost check and a cost analysis of the tender. Explanations will not be difficult to find for any substantial differences. Errors on the part of the surveyor or builder's estimator can occur, and there will be those occasions where the estimator deliberately distorted some of his prices. If there is a trend throughout all the elements, this must be reported accordingly to the client.

Once the contract is signed it is sometimes assumed that the cost planning process has been concluded. The design has stayed within the budget and this is evidenced by an agreeable tender sum. If the client is to be fully satisfied with the costing methods, he will now require the final account to come within this budget figure. This means that the quantity surveyor should price the architect's variations before they are issued to the contractor, so that design decisions are not taken without the full knowledge of any cost implications.

Cost reports, or financial statements as they are sometimes called, should be prepared at regular intervals to keep both the client and the architect aware of the expected final account sum. These constitute cost checking, and have the advantage that the quantity surveyor is now dealing with real contract prices rather than simply his own interpretations, as was the case during the design cost planning process.

On the basis of the following data calculate the elemental costs for the proposed building for: (1) roof; (2) staircase; (3) external walls.

AVAILABLE ANALYSIS
Gross internal floor area = $970 \, m^2$
Cost index 326

	Total cost £	Cost/m^2 gifa £
Roof		
Area $485 \, m^2$		
U-value = 0.6	9750.00	10.05
Staircase		
I Nr rise 3.00 m		
width 1.60 m	1100.00	1.13
Reinforced concrete		
straight flight with		
mild steel balustrade		
and vinyl handrail		
External walls		
U-value = 0.4	8500.00	8.76
comprising $320 \, m^2$ cavity wall		
$80 \, m^2$ cavity wall		

PROPOSED PROJECT
Roof U-value = $0.5 \, W/m^2 \, °C$
Staircases 2 Nr rise 2.80 m, width 1.40 m reinforced concrete with mild steel balustrade and hardwood handrail.
Walls 275 mm cavity with U-value = $0.3 \, W/m^2 \, °C$
Cost index 384

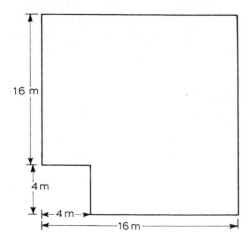

16 m

Two-storey building total wall height 6.50 m

4 m

4 m

16 m

The following effects should be considered:

(1) Market conditions. In practice reference could be made to the Building Cost Information Service index of tender price levels, or locally to any data recorded by the firm.

(2) Type of contract. Some adjustment in practice would be needed if the tenders were not obtained on the same basis, e.g. selected or negotiated tender.

(3) Fluctuations. On the basis of the index numbers above, costs would appear to be rising. The original cost analysis will have been prepared on the tender sum and any other costs recouped in the normal way. It would be assumed that both contracts include a price-fluctuation clause. It should be remembered that cost analyses are prepared on tenders received rather than on final accounts because

(a) accounts are not easy to analyse because of variations.
(b) the data in accounts is much more outdated.

(4) Competitive tender list. No information is available on the number of tenders received or how competitive they were. The difference between tender prices would be carefully noted.

(5) Regional trend. The variation in price between regions could be established using the BCIS regional data statistics.

Roof

Analysis of previous data

Description	Total cost	Cost/m^2 GIFA	Quantity factor	Unit rate
U-value = 0.6	£9750	£10.05	485 m^2	£20.10

The above data can be taken directly from the information provided with the exception of the unit rate. This is obtained by dividing the quantity factor (roof area) into the total cost.

Projected costs

The roof area is calculated as 384 m². A more accurate analysis could have been provided if the lengths of eaves and gutters had been available from the original analysis.

The unit rates calculated from the given data need to be adjusted to take account of the change in U-value from 0.6 to 0.5 W/m²°C (0.5 is better insulated, 0.6 is the maximum permissible in present-day building regulations). The difference might be achieved by a lightweight insulating material either in addition to the existing construction or by substituting alternative materials. The change in U-value requires the equivalent of about 12 mm extra material such as fibreglass. An allowance of £0.50 is therefore added to the unit rate. This is added to the analysis at present-day prices, and does not therefore need adjustment by indices. The previous data will, however, need updating by using the indices provided. This new rate is then multiplied by the roof quantity factor, to provide us with our elemental cost.

$$\text{Roof area} \times \text{Previous unit rate} \times \text{indices} + \text{extra materials cost} = \text{elemental cost}$$

$$384 \times \left[£20.10 \times \frac{384}{326} + £0.50 \right] = £9285 \text{ Roof element.}$$

Staircase

Previous analysis
There is one staircase in the analysis and this has a rise of 3.00 m and a width of 1.50 m. There are several ways in which the cost could be apportioned, all of which, because of the minimum amount of data available, are likely to be subjective. Therefore an assumed analysis might reflect the following.

Mild steel balustrade and
vinyl handrails 10% = £ 110.00
concrete staircase 90% = £ 990.00
       £1100.00

These are two ways in which to analyse the cost of the staircase structure:

(1) Determine the number of steps in the staircase. The riser of a step must not exceed 190 mm for a common staircase, or 220 m for a private staircase. Assess 188 mm as the possible rise gives us 16 steps $\frac{3.00}{188} = 16$ steps.

There are no landings mentioned, therefore the total length of steps = 16 × 1.60 m = 25.60 m. The cost per linear metre of step, therefore, is shown to be

$$\frac{£990.00}{25.60} = £38.67$$

(2) Determine the cost on the basis of rise × width (see later).

Projected costs

There are two staircases and both these have a rise of 2.80 m and a width of 1.40 m. Using method (1) above the cost of this structure can be calculated as follows.

$$\text{Number of steps} = \frac{2.80}{188} = 15 \times \text{width} = 21.00\,\text{m}.$$

The total width is then multiplied by the cost per metre above to give us the cost of the two staircases.

$$2 \times 21.00\,\text{m} \times £38.67 = \underline{\underline{£1624.14}}$$

Adopting method (2) the cost can be calculated as follows.

$$\frac{\text{Width} \times \text{rise in proposed}}{\text{Width} \times \text{rise in analysis}} = \frac{\text{Estimated cost}}{\text{Analysis cost}}$$

$$\frac{2.80 \times 1.40 \times 2}{3.00 \times 1.60} \times £990.00 = \underline{\underline{£1617}}$$

The difference between the two methods is minimal. Method (2) is preferred since the riser height will possibly be greater in the proposed staircase in order to fit in with the overall rise.

Staircase structure	=	£1617.00
Handrails $2 \times \dfrac{2.80}{3.00} \times £110.00$	=	205.33
Say + 10% for hardwood handrail =		20.53
		£1842.86

This sum then needs updating by using the given indices.

$$\text{Staircase element} = 1842.86 \times \frac{384}{326} = \underline{\underline{£2170.73}}$$

External walls

The type of building is unknown, therefore the proportion of this element to be allocated as windows and external doors must be assumed to be similar in both cases.

Area of external walls in the proposed building = $(20.00 + 20.00) \times 2 \times 6.50 = 520\,\text{m}^2$.

External walling to floor ratio of the existing building =

$$\frac{320 + 80}{970} = 0.412.$$

No adjustment for shape can be made since this is unknown in the original building.

Gross floor area of the proposed building = $768\,\text{m}^2$. Therefore $768\,\text{m} \times 0.412 = 316\,\text{m}^2$ external walling in the proposed project.

In the original analysis two types of external walling construction are used. Their individual costs are not, however, shown and they can only be obtained by interpolation. Assume current values for the 275 m cavity wall to be £25/m^2 and for the 375 m cavity wall £34/m^2.

Let the 275 m cavity wall = 25 × 320 m^2 = 8000
Let the 375 m cavity wall = 34 × 80 m^2 = 2720
$$\overline{10720}$$

Therefore the appropriate rates for these two types of walling can be determined as follows.

275 m wall
$$\frac{£\ 8500}{10720} \times 8000 = 6343.28 \div 320\,m^2 = £19.82$$

375 m wall
$$\frac{£\ 8500}{10720} \times 2720 = 2156.72 \div 80\,m^2 = £26.96$$

$$check = £8500.00$$

The cost of the external walling can therefore be determined as follows.

Wall area × unit rate × indices = element cost =

$$412\,m^2 \times £19.82 \times \frac{384}{326} = £9618.66$$

The change in the 'U' value can to some extent be achieved by using a less dense concrete block on the internal skin of the wall. The final element cost can therefore be shown as

$$£9618.66$$

plus extra cost of blocks
at today's prices 412 m^2 × £0.75 = $\underline{309.00}$
$$£9927.66$$

To what building type do you consider the accompanying cost analysis (see over) might refer? Give reasons to support your answer, quantifying them where necessary.

Gross internal floor area

This is the total enclosed space fulfilling the functional requirements of the building, measured between the internal face of the external walls but over any internal walls. This total floor area can be approximately calculated by adding together the substructure and upper floors area i.e. 2013 m^2 + 53 m^2 = 2066 m^2. A more precise figure can be obtained by dividing the total cost by the cost per square metre of gross internal floor area.

$$\frac{£324.167}{£156.53} = 2071\,m^2$$

The reason for this minor discrepancy may be staircase areas which would be absent from the upper floors' quantity factors.

Number of storeys

The building is largely single-storey with a small proportion in two-storey construction (3 per cent). The ground floor area represents 2013 m² and upper floors 53 m².

Height

The maximum building height can be calculated by dividing the volume (heat source) by the ground floor area. This is sufficiently accurate where the second or subsequent floors are the same area. Storey heights, where they are equal, can be obtained by dividing this overall height by the number of floors. The average height could therefore be obtained on the following basis.

$$\frac{\text{Heat source}}{\text{GIFA}} = \frac{11\,916}{2071} = 5.75\,\text{m}$$

This may indicate that parts of the building would exceed this height and parts may represent a typical height for offices of 2.40 m. Assuming that the 53 m² represents the two-storey section at this height, the remaining height can be calculated as follows.

$$\frac{11\,916 - (2 \times 53 \times 2.40)}{2071 - 53 \times 53} = 5.94\,\text{m}$$

Wall-to-floor ratio

This is calculated by dividing the external wall area by the gross floor area to three decimal places.

$$\text{Wall/floor ratio} = \frac{\text{external walls + windows \& external doors}}{\text{gross internal floor area}}$$

$$= \frac{1469\,\text{m}^2 + 46\,\text{m}^2}{2071\,\text{m}^2} = 0.73$$

The lower the ratio, the more economical the design shape.

Building type

Note to candidates: the decision on the building type is probably best approached on the basis of some form of elimination procedure. Assuming that the cost analysis has been prepared in accordance with the BCIS rules, it should relate only to a single building, and not a contract requiring the erection of several buildings. Where several buildings of the same type are constructed and the analysis is for one of them, this should be stated.

The CI/SfB classification is given, and although this will identify the project type, it is unlikely that under examination conditions students will be able to remember such classification numbers.

Although the overall cost per square of gross floor area is given, it is unlikely that this will be particularly helpful since the data are so outdated. Candidates should, however, have a general idea of such building costs and this, coupled with approximate rises in construction costs, may provide some confirmation of the type of project finally selected.

SUMMARY OF ELEMENT COSTS

Gross internal floor area:

Tender date: (1) 26th November 1974

Element	Preliminaries shown separately				Preliminaries apportioned amongst elements		
	Total cost of element £	Cost per m² gross floor area £	Element unit quantity	Element unit rate £	Total cost of element £	Cost per m² gross floor area £	Cost per m² gross floor area at 1st quarter 1977 £
1. Substructure	£24 096	£11.63	2013 m²	£11.97	£27 274	£13.17	£15.67
2. Superstructure							
2.A. Frame	45 202	21.83	1531 m²	29.53	51 163	24.70	
2.B. Upper floors	1024	0.49	53 m²	19.32	1159	0.56	
2.C. Roof	27 898	13.47	2032 m²	13.73	31 577	15.25	
2.D. Stairs	1315	0.64	–	–	1488	0.72	
2.E. External walls	31 004	14.97	1469 m²	21.11	35 093	16.95	
2.F. Windows & external doors	2342	1.13	46 m²	50.91	2651	1.28	
2.G. Internal walls & partitions	8492	4.10	1585 m²	5.36	9612	4.64	
2.H. Internal doors	3090	1.49	65 m²	47.54	3498	1.69	
Group element total	£120 367	£58.12			£136 241	£65.79	£78.29
3. Internal finishes							
3.A. Wall finishes	14 648	7.07	3920 m²	3.74	16 580	8.00	
3.B. Floor finishes	14 984	7.24	2003 m²	7.48	16 960	8.19	
3.C. Ceiling finishes	7151	3.45	1803 m²	3.97	8094	3.91	
Group element total	£36 783	£17.76			£41 634	£20.10	£23.92

	£	£/m²	Quantity	Rate	£	£/m²	£/m²
4. *Fittings and furnishings*	£5 148	£2.49			£5 827	£2.81	£3.35
5. *Services*							
5.A. Sanitary appliances	1805	0.87	45 No	40.11	2043	0.99	
5.B. Services equipment	–	–			–	–	
5.C. Disposal installations	877	0.42			993	0.48	
5.D. Water installations	836	0.40			946	0.46	
5.E. Heat source	40 000	19.32	11 916 m³	3.36	45 275	21.86	
5.F. Space heating & air treatment	}						
5.G. Ventilating system	–	–			–	–	
5.H. Electrical installations	17 000	8.21			19 242	9.29	
5.I. Gas installations	–	–			–	–	
5.J. Lift & conveyor installations	–	–			–	–	
5.K. Protective installations	147	0.07			166	0.08	
5.L. Communication installations	–	–			–	–	
5.M. Special installations	–	–			–	–	
5.N. Builder's work in connection with services	4713	2.28			5335	2.58	
5.O. Builder's profit and attendance on services	884	0.43			100	0.48	
Group element total	£66 262	£32.00			£75 001	£36.22	£43.10
Sub-total excluding External works, Preliminaries and Contingencies	£252 656	£122.00			£285 977	£138.09	£164.33
6. *External*							
6.A. Site work	17 257	8.33			19 533	9.43	
6.B. Drainage	11 878	5.74			13 445	6.49	
6.C. External services	2323	1.12			2629	1.27	
6.D. Minor building works	2282	1.10			2583	1.25	
Group element total	£33 740	£16.29			£38 190	£18.44	£21.94
Preliminaries	£37 771	£18.24			–	–	
TOTALS (less Contingencies)	£324 167	£156.53			£324 167	£156.53	£186.27

Specification data will always accompany a cost analysis, but they have been omitted. Had data been available, they would have helped in the selection process. The aim of this question, therefore, is to test students' deductive powers in attempting to reach the correct solution. Here are some of the points to consider.

(1) The building is largely single-storey with a minor floor area at first-floor level. Buildings such as flats, offices and hotels can therefore be eliminated.

(2) The total floor area of 2071 m^2 indicates a medium-sized contract equal in floor area to perhaps 25 semi-detached houses.

(3) The approximate storey-height may provide a good indication of the building type. Generally this is calculated as approximately 6 m. This might suggest a warehouse or factory building, possibly a church or even a fire-station. This height is, however, likely to be too large for even fire applicances.

(4) A church building would require extensive fittings and furnishings, but the amount included is too low for this, although this work could be covered by a separate contract. But no church would have 45 sanitary appliances! Such a number could indicate a public type of building.

(5) The standard of finishings indicated by the elemental costs is possibly too high for a warehouse building, and the high number of sanitary fittings would support this opinion.

(6) The amount allocated to siteworks is a considerable proportion of the total cost, and this perhaps indicates large areas for car parking.

In this example, the storey-height is possibly the best clue. Residential, educational, health and administrative buildings do not generally require such high storey heights. Factories, warehouses and religious buildings have been considered but eliminated. The alternative therefore seems to be a recreational building, possibly a sports hall, and this fits all the clues.

6   Cost indices and cost limits

Discuss the statement that the use of indices to forecast future building costs is liable to criticism, and describe the way indices are used in practice.

The object of a cost index is to measure changes in cost from one point of time to another. A base date is selected and any future changes in cost are related to this figure. They are an important item in assisting prediction of future costs.

There are many different types of indices constructed from information recorded in the construction industry. The following are examples of available indices.

(1) Building tender price index (DoE, DQSS)
(2) Road construction tender price index (DoE)
(3) Tender price index (BCIS)
(4) Index of public sector housing (DoE)
(5) Housing cost index (Building)
(6) NEDO formula method (PSA)

The following points should be considered in criticism of the use of index numbers.

(1) Index numbers are a measure of past recorded data. They are extended forwards on the basis that the rhythm experienced in the past will to some extent be projected into the future. This may be fallacious. In addition to using index numbers to predict future performance, experience of trends and some knowledge of likely market conditions must be coupled with the recorded data.
(2) The composition of indices is based upon some typical or average commodities (e.g. components of a house in (5) above). These may either be unrepresentative to some regional locations, or become outdated and untypical of the work they are trying to measure.
(3) Other commodities or components that are outside the scope of the index (because it is an impossible task to include every single item) have price changes that may affect the overall values of the index. For example, the NEDO Formula Indices Series 1, Slate and Tile Roofing makes no mention of slates in the index composition.
(4) Labour cost indices are often constructed on the basis of the minimum agreed rates within the industry. Allowances for bonus payments may be ignored, although some DoE labour indices do make provision for these. (Hence the conflicting remarks made by unions and management when negotiating new pay deals). An index could therefore show a trend in the opposite direction of real labour rates used in industry. It may show, for

example, that labour costs are apparently increasing when they are in real terms decreasing (ignoring inflation).

(5) In order to make realistic comparisons the same item, same quantity and same source should be used for the appropriate components of the index. The difficulty sometimes occurs where an original commodity ceases to exist and inaccuracies can then occur by substituting alternative but appropriate items.

(6) It is difficult to maintain a realistic index over a long period of time due to changes in taste and fashion. A correct balance of items originally, may at a later date prove to be inappropriate.

(7) Inaccuracies will occur in the calculations owing to errors and false returns submitted from users who wish to conceal personal information.

Whilst index numbers are subject to some degree of inaccuracy, for general purposes and uses in the construction industry the levels of inaccuracy are usually tolerable.

Uses in practice

The functions of index numbers are as follows:

(1) To assess the differences in levels of tenders at varying dates.
(2) To adjust past costs of buildings to current prices.
(3) To assess future trends in price levels.

In selecting a particular index for practical use, it must be assumed that the surveyor will select the correct and most appropriate index. In order to use it effectively he should known how it has been constructed. He should ensure that it is used only for the purpose that it was intended. He should also ensure that the results achieved are reasonable and that there are no underlying factors that should have been considered. The following are the more common uses of construction cost indices.

(1) Establishing the level of individual tenders.
(2) Adjustment for time-scale.
(3) Cost planning.
(4) Formula method of price adjustment.
(5) Forecasting.
(6) Pricing.
(7) Cash-flow projections.
(8) General comparisons.

Discuss whether the system of cost limits gives value for money in the public sector.

Cost limits have been used for a large number of public construction projects. Their object is to establish a system limiting the expenditure on initial construction costs, but at the same time requiring a minimum standard of accommodation and specification.

Hospital buildings

Hospital buildings should be designed on the basis of cost limits varying with the type of hospital project to be constructed and the number of bed spaces to be provided. Allowances are added for the communication space required within the hospital. The amount allowed for this is subject to fluctuation but is approximately 15 per cent. Abnormal costs can be added based upon the individual project to take account of: external works, height over four storeys, auxiliary buildings, and other factors such as site conditions and air conditioning.

Education buildings

Since the Second World War, there has been a steady process of refinement of layout, economy of specification, dual use of space and an elimination of waste in school buildings. Cost limits were determined by the type of school and the net cost allowed per place. Amounts to cover abnormal conditions were added as lump sums to these net costs per place. The Department of Education and Science ceased to apply formal limits to educational buildings in July 1974, and in their place allocated lump sum authorisations. Local authorities were then expected to obtain the best value in the light of local conditions.

Local authority housing

The current housing programme includes new housing, raising the existing housing standards, building at higher densities and making provision for cars and handicapped and aged persons. Consideration is also given to the more costly pedestrian-segregated layouts. Housing cost yardsticks were first introduced in 1963 to keep down the costs of buildings, so as to reduce the burden to the taxpayer, ratepayer and tenant. The cost limits were related to dwelling conforming to Parker-Morris standards. Additions to the cost limits were made for elderly persons, additional approved amenities, regional price variations and adverse site conditions.

The following points about value for money should be considered.

(1) Cost limits are primarily concerned with initial building costs and not total costs in use. It could be argued, therefore, that they give very poor value for money in the long term. Certainly there is a greater emphasis today to improve the initial design in order to reduce, minimise or eliminate some future cost.

(2) In the absence of cost limits, housing standards and expenditure could reach high and unacceptable proportions. This could result in a substantial reduction in the housing programme (because a limited amount of cash is available for housing), with a consequent lengthening of housing waiting lists, or large rent increases to both new and existing tenants.

(3) In order to build within the prescribed limits, increased site densities may become necessary. This may result in more three/four storey blocks being constructed. These have the disadvantages that they are more expensive to construct initially than equivalent two-storey dwellings, are more costly to manage and maintain and are also less desirable to tenants.

(4) Cost limits are one of the reasons for refinement of layout, economy of specification and the elimination of waste in the design of many publicly-financed building projects. In order for schemes to obtain approval, design layouts and appearance had to be more carefully thought out.

(5) Unrealistic cost limits, which have been common in more recent years, produce poor-performance buildings, stereotyped solutions and poor elevational considerations.

On balance it can be argued that the introduction of cost limits for public buildings was essential in order to achieve an economical design, but it is unlikely that their constant use will refine the design to any greater extent. In practice there has been an emphasis on producing designs in modern times not to a rigid cost limit but more with costs in use in mind.

Describe the factors to be considered in the construction of index numbers.

Indices are a way of expressing the change in cost of a particular item or group of items over a period of time. These changes are related to a base year which is a point in time against which all other similar costs can be compared. There are several mathematical formulae that may be used for constructing an index. An index, for example, may be obtained by using quantities obtained from the base year as weights. This is known as a Laspayres index and is the type commonly used in practice in the construction industry. An alternative approach is to use quantities obtained from the year under consideration; this is known as a Paasche index. The comparison of the price of an item in one time period relative to another time period is known as a price relative.

When constructing an index, the following factors will need to be examined.

Purpose of the index

This requires careful consideration because it is fundamental to all of the other factors. Correct interpretation of the index can only be made when its purpose is fully understood. This is particularly important in these days since indices are constructed for almost everything that can be measured. The number of index numbers within the construction industry, for example, is now considerable. One may be forgiven for assuming that a building cost index and a tender price index are measuring one and the same thing i.e. the increases in the costs of construction. The building cost index measures the costs to the contractor whereas the tender price index measures the costs to the client. The latter includes the constractor's profit, the former does not. Several sub-divisions of each of these indices are available in an attempt to measure the work more precisely. A further point is that an index constructed to represent the costs of timber in buildings cannot be used, for example, to measure the price of brickwork. It may provide an overall indication of a general trend for all building materials but it cannot be used to provide any form of realistic assessment.

Selection of items

This can be one of the most difficult problems of all in formulating the index. The correct solution often lies in defining carefully the purpose of the index and then choosing those items that best achieve that purpose. The items selected must be properly representative of the work that they are trying to describe, otherwise inaccurate forecasts and updating will be made. Two conflicts also occur. In order to be as representative as possible a large number should be included; but because of the costs necessary in collecting and revising the index, the number of items should be kept to a minimum. It may be found that a few well-chosen items will adequately measure the changes that occur. Only items with a long future ahead should be selected. The substitution of items for those that are no longer available can cause distortions in the index, and make forecasts less accurate.

Choice of weights

In order for an index to have any value the items must be weighted in respect of their proportional importance. Indices are therefore generally constructed on the basis of the 'basket of goods' approach. For example, if we were trying to assemble an index for houses, brickwork would be more important than, say, gully pots, and would therefore be weighted accordingly. If the purpose has been clearly defined and the correct selection of items made, the allocation of weights should be straighforward. Although weighting is important, the actual values allocated do not apparently make a great deal of difference within the index.

Choice of base year

The base year of the index should be a typical year when no unusual events occurred. The choosing of a freak year would result in a misleading series of index numbers being prepared. Base years are usually designated in order to allow for increases or decreases that may occur in subsequent years.

Methods of construction

Index numbers can be constructed for almost any process that is changing over a period of time. The two most useful indices applicable to quantity surveying are probably the Building Cost Indices and the Tender Price Indices. In practice several variations of these are available. A building cost index measures the costs of the builder. It is commonly known as a factor cost index, and is based upon the measurement of the contractors' resources such as wages, material prices and plant costs. These factors have themselves their own index which is used to compile the building cost index. The tender price index is based upon the cost to the client and therefore attempts to take into account the tendering market conditions. By pricing a typical bill of quantities and then repricing at some future date, we can construct an index to show how building prices have changed during the period under examination.

7 Cost comparisons

Discuss the opinion that an office block without windows would be more economic than one constructed with windows.

To answer this question requires the consideration of the total costs in use of this element and the influence of this element on the other affected elements. The function of a window is to allow adequate natural light into buildings and also to ventilate rooms. The implications of the building regulations requirements regarding ventilation would therefore need to be examined. Windows, including the treatment around their openings, must be weather-proof. They must also provide for adequate security and their thermal transmittance should be kept to a minimum. The following points should be considered.

(1) A comparison between the initial costs of the external wall construction and the window costs (per square metre). This might typically have a ratio of 2:1 (walls to windows).

(2) The recurring costs associated with windows will be higher than those for external walls. Regular cleaning of windows will be necessary and damage due to accidental breakage will need to be allowed. In addition, depending upon the type of window framing used, repairs and replacement will be a consideration. If brickwork were to be used for external walling, then the only real maintenance aspects would be its repointing as and when required, perhaps every 20 years.

(3) Artificial lighting is normally switched on for most of the time in offices, because of the high illumination required. A suggestion might therefore be made to operate the entire lighting of the office from a minimum number of switches. This would initially provide some savings in switches and cables, and in use because lamps could last longer. An improved emergency lighting system will become more important, because in times of electricity failure the natural lighting would not be available either to allow some work to be continued or to provide for evacuation from the building.

(4) The omission of windows could mean that better ventilation and air conditioning will be needed. However, in many office blocks the windows are already fixed lights, and the ventilation is achieved by mechanical means.

(5) Heat loss through windows is greater than the heat loss through external walls. A saving could therefore be achieved in recurring fuel costs, and because the amount of heat produced could therefore be reduced, a saving in the provision of the components (heat source and distribution) required for the heating system could be made.

(6) There will possibly be less damage due to vandalism. This may in turn have the effect of reducing insurance premiums.

(7) Although the security of the building will be improved, due to the reduced number of possible entry points, any forced entry would be more

difficult to detect. However, the costs of a security system could possibly be reduced.

(8) In parallel with this last point, the fire premiums might be higher because an outbreak of fire would also be less easy to detect. A proper fire alarm system would, however, tend to compensate for this.

An office block constructed without windows is a more economic proposition than one with windows. Financial savings would be achieved in the initial costs of the windows (after allowing for the costs of additional external walling) and the heating components. There would also be savings in the recurring costs of building maintenance and heating-fuel costs. Increased spending would be necessary for the higher lighting costs (some allowance would normally be made for the natural light contribution) both initially (for increased lighting equipment) and in use. Some increases may be necessary for the costs of improved mechanical ventilation, although this is unlikely, unless natural ventilation was to be partially relied upon in the normal building.

In the context of 'a more economic proposition', other factors such as the social and aesthetic conditions will also need to be considered. People tend to work better and more productively, and are more content, in pleasant surroundings. A further factor is that, in the absence of any windows, the client or developer may find that the building is unsaleable, or difficult to let.

A client is proposing to construct an office building. He has two alternatives in mind. One is based upon a traditional cellular layout whereas the other is of an open-plan design. Discuss the economic considerations of these alternatives.

This question can be answered under three headings.

Initial construction costs

The open-plan layout has an obvious cost advantage for certain elements (internal walls and partitions, internal doors and internal wall finishes), simply because of their exclusion from the design. Omitting these items could result in a 20 per cent saving on the initial construction costs. The open-plan layout may, however, result in a more expensive floor and roof construction because of the longer spans necessary, due to less internal support. This could be offset by the introduction of isolated columns within the structural design. Without the use of these columns, the external walls and their foundations may need to be of a more robust construction resulting in higher costs for these elements. The elements, stairs, windows and external doors and other internal finishes should be largely unaffected.

The costs of plumbing installation, lifts and electrical installation are likely to be only marginally different. Communication installations will in practice probably cost about the same in each case. The ventilation system (air conditioning), which has almost become an essential feature of new office buildings, can be of a simpler design and layout in the open-plan building.

The type of heating installation that might be suitable for the traditional cellular designed office may be unsuitable in the open-plan offices. An alternative heating system, such as ducted warm air, may be more appropriate. Further consideration will be necessary protective installations, e.g. fire-fighting, in the open-plan design.

Costs in use

If the client plans to use the building himself, he will be particularly interested in the recurring costs of running, repair and replacement. His attitude to these factors will, of course, be different if he is developing the proposed site for a sale or lease. He will, however, need to consider these costs in this context, otherwise he may find the property difficult to dispose of.

The Building Maintenance Cost Information Service provides occupancy cost analysis data for buildings in use. Consideration should be given to decorations, repairs of the building fabric, fuels, maintenance and renewal of the engineering services, cleaning and items such as security, rubbish removal and insurance.

The costs of redecoration, for example, are likely to be less expensive in the open-plan office (because of reduced wall area). Fuel costs for heating may be less expensive in the cellular building because the internal division walls will provide some form of insulation. The need to provide more expensive engineering services for the cellular building will also result in higher maintenance costs in use.

Usage factors

In recent years, there has been a trend towards the open-plan design. A cellular design may therefore be thought of as being old-fashioned and could be difficult to dispose of, if constructed by a speculative developer. One assumes that the external plan dimensions of the two buildings are the same. This would result in the net internal floor area (usable floor area) being higher in the open-plan design.

The quantity surveyor should also be able to indicate the likely effects on the employees' productivity of the alternative design proposals. Opinions vary, and it is important to try and obtain data relating to the specific type of office use contemplated.

It can be shown that more pleasant working conditions tend to increase employee productivity, and the esteem of the company concerned.

The open-plan design will also provide more flexibility in use.

Conclusions

The choice of either of the alternatives suggested will be a matter for the client to decide. He may already have his preference, and anyway, it is not the quantity surveyor's role to try and change the client's mind. The quantity surveyor should, however, be able to make a reliable comparison based upon methods of construction, information available and known trends that may influence the costs in use.

Explain the factors which you would take into account when advising a property owner whether to refurbish a building, demolish it and redevelop the site or do only essential repairs.

It might be assumed that redevelopment of premises will always take place if adequate funds can be made available. One reason to support this opinion is that of the inherent obsolescence of old buildings. They were designed for another age and have become outdated because of the new technologies now available. Older buildings were not generally better constructed than are modern structures. Perhaps one reason for retaining an old building is that of its historic character and association. This is particularly true of listed buildings, or buildings of special architectural interest where planning restrictions are in force. There may also be planning restrictions that could limit the wholesale redevelopment of a particular site.

Essential repairs are assumed to mean minimal repairs which are undertaken where funds do not permit otherwise, or where compulsory redevelopment is contemplated in the very near future.

In deciding whether to refurbish, redevelop or carry out only essential repairs, the following factors need to be considered.

Condition

The existing condition of the building would need to be surveyed. If the structure was sound, refurbishment might be considered. If it was very dilapidated, demolition would probably be the only realistic course of action. This might occur where the structure has been allowed to deteriorate over a number of years beyond useful renovation. Where the building is in very good repair, and age is not a factor to consider, essential repairs only may be contemplated.

Location

Are the existing premises in the correct location for the users, or would alternative accommodation in a new position be more appropriate? In this case, it may be preferable to try and sell the site for possible redevelopment by others, and undertake no work other than to ensure the safety of the building. If the building is in an area that is becoming run down, it may be inappropriate to consider refurbishment, should compulsory purchase be a consideration of the local authority. Alternatively, if it is important for, say, business reasons to stay in the present location, redevelopment or refurbishment may be essential.

Maintenance and repairs

Some funds will have already been spent on maintaining the existing building. There may come a time, however, when the costs associated with maintenance become so high that an alternative course of action becomes necessary. This will become apparent particularly if in the foreseeable future expensive repairs will be required. The owner will then be faced with the choice of either large-scale refurbishment or complete redevelopment. Generally speaking, modern buildings should be easier and therefore less expensive to maintain.

Running costs

The costs of using engineering services may be considerable. Where systems have been in use for a number of years, they may be both uneconomic and unreliable for today's use. For example, a heating system may, in addition to being old-fashioned and awkward in operation, also be inefficient and technically outdated. It may require considerable fuel to provide a suitable room temperature in order to combat heat loss both because of poor insulation qualities and outmoded design of the building. Replacement of the engineering services will eventually become necessary, and at this point the question of at least some modernisation will need to be examined.

Continuity of use

A major disadvantage of complete redevelopment is the disruption of normal processes, even where suitable alternative accommodation can be found close by. In business, a temporary loss of clients could be expected. Housing communities may be uprooted and destroyed. The advantage of refurbishment or modernisation is that the work can generally be phased, and although some inconvenience will occur, this is likely to be only temporary, with business carrying on 'as usual' and communities finally being restored. This may also be an important factor in trying to find out the wishes of future occupiers.

Grants and taxation

The importance of these two factors will influence the decision to be made. Whereas the costs of maintenance of buildings can be offset against company taxation, the costs of new buildings generally cannot, except in certain situations. If grants are available towards the costs of redevelopment, this may sway the choice from a less expensive refurbishment project. Grants may also be obtainable from central government in respect of industrial buildings for some locations.

Expected life

The expected life (or remaining life) of the building will have some influence on the decision, particularly where refurbishment is being contemplated. Adequate refurbishment will have the effect of extending this life. There must be a point, however, when the useful life of a building ceases, for example, when it becomes uneconomic to maintain or unsuitable because of its design, for all practical purposes.

Space

Older buildings do not make the best possible use of space for modern-day use. In order to adapt a building for today's processes, refurbishment may become so extensive as to make redevelopment a better alternative. Better use of space can often be achieved by a completely new design. If the existing space available is insufficient, the possibility of extending the premises may be considered. If space around the site does not permit this approach, some form of redevelopment may become essential. Modern buildings are also generally more adaptable.

Appearance

The existing external appearance of a building can be an important consideration where it is intended to portray an image of the occupiers. If it is not possible to redesign an elevation to meet the owner's requirements, this may be a good reason for redevelopment.

Demolition

The costs of demolishing the existing building will also need to be considered. If there is an adjoining property, some form of structural support may be needed to protect it during demolition and reconstruction. Salvaged materials arising from the demolition can sometimes be used to offset the costs of demolition.

In considering how to approach this problem, the condition of the existing building is likely to be a major influencing factor. The costs of repairs and maintenance, together with running costs, should be examined carefully, remembering that eventually major work will need to be undertaken in these areas to equip the building to current standards. If continuity of use is of prime importance, then phased refurbishment will be a proper course of action. It should also be remembered that refurbishment will generally be completed more quickly than will a new development project.

Suggest the reasons why flats in multi-storey blocks are more expensive than comparative accommodation in low-rise dwellings.

This question is concerned with the costs associated with construction at various overall building heights. Tall buildings are never selected for cost reasons and are overall more expensive for the following reasons:

(1) The higher constructional costs arising from building at a higher level. These are the costs associated with vertical transportation, including the provision of cranes and hoists, the difficulties of materials storage, the increased amounts payable to operatives and the safety requirements.

(2) The increased costs of engineering services not present in low-rise dwellings, including space for their provision within the structure e.g. mechanical passenger lifts, refuse-disposal installations, pumping equipment for water services, special equipment for sewage disposal, protective installations such as fire fighting and lightening conductors.

(3) The higher costs of provision for certain elements, e.g. foundations (possibility of introducing piling), the requirements of a structural frame, more stringent construction of staircases, provision of more fittings and furnishings for compactness and the increased costs of engineering services described above.

(4) An increase in the proportion of circulation areas required, including wider stairways, larger landing areas, areas for access, clothes-drying facilities and access areas for the engineering services.

(5) The improvement of fire-resistance precautions, particularly insulation between floor levels.

(6) Less competition because of the limited number of building contractors capable of undertaking the work. Although some contractors became specialists with these types of projects, their tender prices reflected their competitors.

(7) New and experimental forms of construction in the 1960s tended to increase uncertainties of performance, and required large expenditure on specialised mechanical plant, which resulted in higher prices.

(8) Because of the complexities involved, more of the work had to be awarded to specialist nominated subcontractors. The only exception to the fact that tall buildings are more expensive is the possible provision of one or two extra storeys in order to make the best use of passenger lifts and other expensive engineering services. Multi-storey buildings may therefore be selected on the basis of a minimal land cost and for speed of construction. They do have some cost advantages, e.g. with the roof.

Two- to four-storey blocks are marginally less expensive than houses and bungalows, for the following reasons:

(1) The foundations to houses and bungalows can support greater loads than they in fact do, and some economy is therefore achieved by this cost being shared by more dwellings.

(2) A similar argument can be used in connection with the roofing costs. The element cost of the roof for a four-storey four-flat block may equate with that of a bungalow of equal floor area. This shows that the element cost per flat represents only a quarter of that of a bungalow. The same argument cannot be directly applied to tall blocks of flats where different design and constructional methods are contemplated.

(3) The floor areas of flats are often lower than those for houses or bungalows equipped for the same numbers of people. The costs per square metre of gross internal floor area on the latter group may therefore be more economical than the low-rise block of flats.

(4) Single-storey dwellings are particularly expensive because they do not make the best possible use of foundations and roofs. The costs of houses alone may show the minimal cost when compared with all other types of dwellings.

(5) There is an overall preference for houses and bungalows, and social costs should also be considered.

A client has the option of providing equivalent accommodation in either (a) one 12-storey block; (b) two six-storey blocks or (c) three four-storey blocks. Advise the client on the ecnomic considerations of these alternative superstructures.

The best method of approaching this problem is to undertake some form of elemental analysis for the three alternative designs. The details of the construction are unknown so we are examining principles only. The costs of substructures have to be ignored as far as this question is concerned.

Frame

The first factor to consider is the necessity for a frame. Load-bearing walls can possibly be used for the four-storey block, eliminating the need for a frame and so providing some cost advantage in these blocks. The six-storey blocks might best use a frame, although this will be a more slender section than the one required for the twelve-storey block. The cost of the frame, for this reason and also due to greater hoisting and fixing requirements, makes the twelve-storey block the most expensive in both total cost and cost per square metre of floor area. Other factors that should be considered are: the choice of steel or concrete, pre-cast or in-situ, time taken for erection of the framework (steel is the quickest), requirements for hoisting, fire protection required, costs of transportation of prefabricated members, safety factors in design and construction, repetition and maintenance. The spacing of the framework grid will have an important effect upon cost.

Upper floors

The cost of this element varies directly with the rate of change in the ratio of upper floor area to total area. For this reason this element will be more expensive in the twelve-storey block since it has a greater number of upper floors (twelve-storey block – eleven upper floors; two six-storey blocks – ten; three four-storey blocks – nine), and hence a greater area. As with some other elements it is necessary to consider the relationship with other elements to fully evaluate the solution. Factors to consider are methods of construction, loadings and floor spans.

Roof

The percentage of the total cost of a building which is used for the roof element will be roughly inversely proportional to the number of storeys. The four-storey blocks will be the most expensive since they will require, in total, three times the area compared with the single twelve-storey block and 50 per cent more than the six-storey blocks.

Stairs

Staircase construction costs depend upon the materials used, shape, width, and storey height, and should also include in their analysis details of the surrounding walls. About two-thirds of the total cost of a concrete staircase are allocated to finishes and balustrades. One staircase will be required in a two-storey building, and the need for fire escapes above three storeys makes two staircases mandatory. When considering costs it is worth remembering that there is one less flight than there are number of storeys. This would require flights in the same ratio as upper floors.

External walls

The cost of this element varies according to the plan size and shape and the number of storeys and overall height. The type and size of openings in the external walls can also affect the elemental cost. The construction may be either load-bearing or as infill to a frame. Generally, buildings above four storeys would be built with a framework. The thickness and type of wall are usually determined by factors other than strength or stability, such as weather exclusion and thermal insulation. The areas of external walling in each of the three schemes should be approximately equal. Any difference in costs is therefore likely to be attributable to scaffolding and height factors, and so make this element in the twelve-storey block the most expensive.

Window and external doors

The ratio of this element area to the floor area in a building varies considerably. There will be a greater number of external doors in the four-storey block, although the numbers of windows should remain constant throughout. Provision may need to be made for the easy cleaning of windows or the provision of cradles in the taller blocks. The differences in costs of this element will be minimal between the alternatives suggested.

Internal partitions

The absence of layout plans makes this element difficult to evaluate. Partitions are greatly affected by changes in plan, although the nature of this effect is difficult to assess because it depends so much upon the type of building under examination. Increased circulation and service areas are likely with the taller blocks and as such make the twelve-storey block marginally the most expensive as far as this element is concerned.

Internal finishes

There should be no apparent differences in the costs of finishings because the floor areas and specification should be almost identical. A contractor may suggest higher rates on the taller blocks for hoisting of materials and vertical transportation of labour but in these comparisons it should only be marginal.

Engineering services

Minor differences in the costs of plumbing, heating and electrical work would be envisaged. Separate incoming mains will be required making the four-storey blocks marginally more expensive. This will be offset by the special considerations and equipment necessary in the twelve-storey blocks regarding water pumps, refuse and waste disposal.

The major differences in services are likely to be in the provision of lifts and their associated shafts and motor rooms. The three four-storey blocks will each require a lift whereas the twelve-storey block may need only one lift, depending upon the floor area served. The costs of the lift installation include the cars, gates, wire ropes, lifting gear and control equipment. These costs will be influenced by the number of floors served, speed, load and form of control. Should the twelve-storey block need two lifts, this will make it the most expensive alternative.

Other factors

Assuming the same site, the external works to the twelve-storey block will be more extensive, but this may have the advantage of providing more car parking areas and open spaces than can be made available on the other blocks. Alternatively, a smaller site can be used with a saving in land charges. Longer lengths of drain trench and an increase in the number of manholes will be expected with the four-storey blocks. Some consideration towards preliminary costs should be given and these are likely to be influenced by construction time rather than any other factors. The taller block may require a tower crane whereas the four-storey block could possibly be erected by use of less expensive plant.

Generally

Examination of the above factors on a cost analysis basis would indicate the twelve-storey block to be the most expensive, and this would only be chosen on the assumption of a restricted site area.

You are currently carrying out a cost-planning function for a proposed block of flats. The client has suggested using asphalt on either in-situ concrete or precast concrete units in preference to felt on timber joists for the roof construction. Comment upon the cost implications of these different methods of construction.

This question considers the provision of reliable cost information based upon a cost study of alternative methods of construction. The amount of detail expected in an answer may require the use of some form of approximate quantities together with a knowledge of appropriate building prices. The life expectancy of the materials used and any maintenance costs expected should also be considered. The quantity surveyor should be able to provide some cost advice taking into account the span of structural members, thermal requirements and other aspects, including the provision of a vapour barrier and the necessity for falls on the roof. The use of different decking materials for the timber structures can influence both the size of softwood joists and the centres to which they will be placed. The introduction of laminated joists will assist towards longer spans, and the provision of timber or steel beams at mid-span will encourage smaller-sized sections. Steel reinforcing bars are preferable to fabric mesh in the concrete structure and on large schemes this will become a necessary alternative.

The structural components should be adequate for the life of building, assuming that correct constructional principles have been used, e.g. treatment of timber against rot and insect attack. The coverings used will, however, need some remedial work if one assumes the life of the building to be at least 60 years. Bituminous felt roof coverings may on average need replacement every 15 years, although this period can be extended by regular maintenance every five years. The asphalt roof coverings should provide a much longer period of trouble-free life and their renewal may be expected every 30 years.

The use of other types of flat roof coverings should not automatically be discounted, and materials such as aluminium, copper or lead, although having a first-cost disadvantage, should provide an almost maintenance-free roof finish for in excess of 100 years. Perhaps these materials are more vulnerable to theft rather than the weather, and although this may be a matter for the insurance company, 'lead' clauses may require the payment of a higher premium annually.

Some consideration should also be given to the alternative constructional details at the eaves and abutments, for forming gutters and finishing around rooflights. These are likely to have only a marginal influence upon the overall costs of the scheme, and are unlikely to be a major factor in the selection process.

The following table shows a comparison between roof structure and roof-covering costs expressed in indices form, to avoid the necessity for actual costs becoming outdated. Where an index range is shown this represents different qualities of the same material.

Roof structure	Index
Reinforced concrete 125 mm thick including reinforcement, formwork, insulating screed and vapour barrier.	410
Pre-stressed concrete beams, insulating screed and vapour barrier	400
Hollow tile construction, ditto	420
175 × 50 softwood joists, firring pieces, insulation, vapour barrier and 50 mm woodwool slabs	270
Ditto with channel reinforced slabs	330
Ditto with 18 mm plywood	360
Ditto with 18 mm chipboard	260

The approximate comparative costs of flat roof coverings shown in indices form may be as follows:

Roof coverings	Index
3-layer bituminous felt	100–110
sheet lead. code 3–5	300–500
sheet zinc. 12–14 gauge	300–340
sheet copper. 0.55–0.70 mm	500–600
asphalt	100–140

The cost of removing dilapidated coverings makes felt marginally less expensive than asphalt. If the scrap value of the other materials is considered, their removal could show a positive amount to the client.

The above data indicates the initial costs of using felt roofing and chipboard roof boarding on timber joists to be the the the most economic (460), compared with asphalt on an in-situ concrete construction (510). Using an expensive copper sheeting finish may increase the overall costs of the roof by almost 2½ times. Even when taking into account replacement costs, bituminous felt roofing for flat roofs still has the minimum life-cycle cost.

In practice flat roofs are out of fashion often because of their appearance but more so because they can often be very troublesome. Chipboard and woodwool slabs have the disadvantage that if they become wet they deteriorate permanently and will need replacing. A minor leak in the roof covering, unnoticed by the building's inhabitants, can result in expensive repairs, sometimes out of all proportion to the initial cost saving. For this reason, plywood which is more resilient is recommended. In order to attempt to reduce any possible structural damage, regular, careful maintenance is required. A further disadvantage resulting from these problems is the disturbance that can be caused by having to attend to roof repairs.

Concrete roofs should provide much less problems and less attention will be required to keep the roof in good order. Some consideration may, however, need to be given to the additional self-weight of the concrete structure in lieu of the timber construction. This may cause cost variations to either a frame, if used, or to the load-bearing walls and their respective foundations, and thus further increase the overall initial building costs.

8   Cost studies

Discuss the cost-sensitivity of the roof element in the following:

(1) high-rise luxury flats in a city centre
(2) speculative single-storey warehouse
(3) multi-storey car park
(4) old people's home in a country setting.

The cost-sensitivity of an element is dependent upon its total cost compared with the total cost of the building. Its quantity relative to the gross floor area is therefore very significant. Its quality or performance are only cost-sensitive where the quantity factor of the element is high, and then just how sensitive depends upon the combined costs of other elements. For an element to be cost-sensitive, any substantial change in its cost must significantly affect the total initial building cost.

(1) In a high-rise building, the roof element, regardless of the construction, is unlikely to be in any way a cost-sensitive element. For example, assuming a ten-storey high block of flats, the cost of the roof element will be less than 1 per cent. The greater the number of floor levels, the less important is the cost of the roof. In a luxury block of flats the cost-sensitive elements are more likely to be associated with the appearance and comfort aspects of the design.
(2) The total cost of a building of this nature, at today's prices, may be in the order of £170.00/m^2 for a typical construction. The roof element could easily represent £25.00 which is approximately 15% of the total cost, assuming the use of corrugated sheeting or equivalent. The quantity factor for this element in buildings of this type is high. Because it represents a significant proportion of the total costs, and also because of its quantity factor, any changes in the specification are likely to alter the cost accordingly. It is therefore considered to be a cost-sensitive element for these types of buildings.
(3) It might be arguable at first sight whether such a building has a roof at all. For those car parks where cars park on the roof, no cost would be allocated to this element and the question of cost-sensitivity would be irrelevant. In multi-storey car parks that do incorporate a roof, then some of the comments made in respect of (a) above are relevant. However, it should be remembered that in these types of building they comprise little in the way of windows, doors finishing, services. Even after allowing for the minimal costs associated with these elements the roof element would not be considered cost-sensitive.
(4) This may imply either a single-storey or two-storey building. The roof element will of course be more cost-sensitive in the single-storey building.

Assuming single-storey construction is implied, the roof element using inexpensive materials may represent 12 per cent of the total cost. It should be remembered that, when comparing analysis for different projects, the quantity factor of this element generally represents the flat plan area over the external walls and not the area of the roof slope. The question may imply a higher quality of roof finishing, e.g. natural slates to comply with planning requirements. This will have the effect of increasing the proportion of the costs to the roof element considerably. It is concluded, therefore, that the roof element for this type of building is cost-sensitive.

Show how the costs of heating, lighting and ventilation are affected because of a change in the plan shape of a building.

The shape of a building has an important effect upon cost. The simpler the shape, the lower will be the overall unit cost. When buildings become long and narrow, or the outline shape more complex, an increase in the perimeter to floor ratio can be measured, accompanied by a higher cost. Various types of building such as offices, as well as needing to be cost-effective, need to make the best possible use of the internal layout of accommodation. This factor is often in opposition to the simple plan shape. Hence a rectangular-shaped building may be chosen in preference to the more cost-effective square shape to provide a practical and functional building.

There are situations where the shape of the building is determined by the shape of the site, or factors such as the slope of the site. Long narrow buildings running with the contours will be more cost-effective for foundations than designs requiring large quantities of cut and fill.

Heating

The cost of heating largely depends upon two factors:

(1) The quantity of heat required, which depends chiefly upon the architect's design skill.
(2) The cost per unit, which depends upon the engineer's design skill.

The amount of heat necessary to maintain comfortable living conditions is influenced by the shape and size of the building, the thermal transmittance of the construction, the orientation and degree of exposure and the amount of ventilation provided. A change in any one of these design factors will affect the capital costs of the heat source (the boiler house and plant), the distribution system used (pipes and radiators) and the future maintenance, repair and running costs.

The effects of building plan shape on the cost of heating can therefore be summarised as follows.

The heat loss through walls increases in proportion to the total wall area, and this is dependent upon the plan shape. The heat loss will therefore be greater from more complex plan shapes than from the simple square shapes. More heat will therefore have to be provided for a similar internal floor area, resulting in possibly a larger and therefore more expensive boiler plant. Because many distribution systems for heating follow the perimeter of the building, greater lengths of pipework will be needed, resulting in a higher cost. The larger heating system in the more complex-shaped building will require greater repair and maintenance, and it will also be necessary, owing to more heat being lost through the walls, to allow a greater cost to cover fuel charges.

Lighting

Both the initial and recurring costs of lighting in buildings depend upon the degree of illumination required. This will be greater in buildings such as offices where a high degree of illumination is required. Long narrow buildings make the best possible use of available natural lighting. Large square buildings, which overall are cost-effective, will be unsatisfactory where it is intended to rely upon a natural light source. Taller windows could improve this, but might necessitate greater storey heights. Large areas of windows to provide natural lighting in order to reduce the costs of artificial lighting will need to allow for the provision of blinds in order to reduce glare. Complex plan shapes and the close proximity of tall adjacent buildings will reduce lighting by natural means. The complex plan shapes are likely to require a larger number of lighting points, resulting in greater lengths of cable and conduit and the initial costs of the installation. This will have the added effect of increasing the electricity charges (related loosely to the number of lighting points) and of any subsequent renewal or repair costs.

Ventilation

The costs of ventilation will depend upon whether natural or artifical ventilation is required. The costs of natural ventilation will be affected by the plan shape only to the extent that more windows may be provided, and in turn these may incorporate more opening lights. Artificial ventilation may become a necessity in large square buildings, particularly in their central areas. Where artificial ventilation is to be provided anyway, more ducting will be required as the building moves away from the square shape and hence both initial and running costs will be increased by this proportion.

The inter-relationship between these three engineering services should also be considered. In many circumstances, the plan shape of the building will be in conflict with these services when attempting to achieve the best solution for each element.

List and describe those factors which affect the costs of windows in buildings.

There is a wide range of choices available for windows in buildings, which results in large cost differences in constructional methods adopted, materials used and the type of glazing selected. High-quality windows in aluminium or hardwood in prestige buildings may initially be five times as expensive as the standard metal or wood windows used on housing schemes. Windows are, however, unlikely to be a cost-sensitive element except in those circumstances where a form of curtain walling is adopted.

Materials used

There is a large variety of materials that can be used for the framework, such as softwood, hardwood, steel, aluminium and plastics. Frames made of a good-quality hardwood such as afromosia may be 2½ times as expensive as the similar frame made in softwood. The difference in cost between a softwood casement window and a standard metal window is only marginal.

Manufacture

An important factor to consider is whether to select a standard stock pattern unit or to opt for a purpose-made design. Often in the case of refurbishment work, the architect has no alternative but to select the latter. Using a non-standard size of softwood window may result in an extra 50 per cent being added to the catalogue price. The size of the section framing will also have an effect upon the price.

Performance

Windows described as high performance in weather-proofing, ventilation requirements and manufacturing quality can be substantially more expensive. High-performance characteristics can add 40 per cent to a typical dwelling-type window.

Size

Small windows have a higher cost per square metre than larger ones of a similar construction. This is due both to the cost of manufacturing the window and to forming the opening in the wall. Cost is much more correlated on the basis of window perimeter than window area.

Glazing

The type of glazing selected or required because of the size of the window can have an important influence upon cost. Glazing in small panes might show an increase of 20 per cent over the optimum size. Very large units in single panes are also expensive because of the type of glass required. Sheet glass is the least expensive followed closely by cast and float glass. Georgian wired polished plate glass is almost three times as expensive as ordinary glazing-quality sheet glass. The introduction of double glazing raises the cost even higher. Special types of glazing for safety, security or thermal comfort are at the top end of the range.

Opening lights

This is one of the more important cost factors in window design particularly for high-performance windows. Opening lights cost considerably more than areas of fixed glazing, due to the extra costs of manufacturing the casement, angle jointing and ironmongery which in itself is susceptible to wide variations in price.

Window type

The selection of the window design such as casement, sliding sash, etc. will also be a factor to consider. The style of the window (whether Georgian, or if the window has curved members resulting in curved glazing) will also need to be considered.

Fixing

The method of fixing and any special requirements regarding fixing will need to be included with the analysis. This may require a timber subframe for the steel or aluminium windows. Adopting the BCIS rules for cost analysis the costs of lintels and the treatment to jambs and stills, including finishings, also need to be allowed for to make a realistic comparison. This is particularly the case where an elemental cost is required.

Special requirements

In certain circumstances, special considerations may be necessary when determining the costs of windows. For example, in multi-storey buildings the particular problems of cleaning, reglazing, general maintenance and safety need to be accounted for. Cradles hung from the roof can deal with many of these factors, and in addition, in offices, window ventilators and fixed lights can deal with safety aspects. Alternatively, windows have been designed which can be reversed for cleaning and other purposes.

Costs in use

The costs of provision of double glazing, and the elimination of draughts by efficient weather stripping, can be partially offset by future savings resulting from a reduced heat loss. Life-cycle cost comparisons between various window types have not always been conclusive, particularly where new improved techniques of manufacture are constantly available. Most steel, aluminium and plastic windows are self-finished and require no immediate treatment or future decoration. This provides real savings in both manpower and money. One can't help wondering, however, how such windows might appear in 25 years time. Timber windows have the disadvantage of requiring immediate decoration and also repeating this process at regular intervals. They also have the disadvantage of being susceptible to rot, and their replacement usually involves costs not directly attributable to this factor. The remainder of costs in use associated with windows is attributable to damaged panes either accidently or through vandalism. These occurrences are, however, generally insurable.

Discuss the economic factors to consider in connection with substructures to buildings.

The type and size of foundations required for a building are influenced by the type of construction, subsequent usage and the bearing capacity of the ground. The other factors which influence the foundation cost are the soil conditions, the water table level in the ground, the type of plant that can be utilised, the slope of the ground and the amount of cut and fill required. Detailed information on subsoil conditions is a prerequisite in choosing the most suitable and economical type of foundation. Large buildings and awkward sites will always justify the cost of a proper site investigation. A two-storey dwelling on good ground strata should only require a foundation depth of 750 mm. In areas of shrinkable clay, short-bored piling can be competitive with traditional strip foundations, and these are much less expensive than a deep strip foundation. In good virgin ground, trench fill methods of construction should be an economical option, although special care needs to be exercised on site. Raft foundations are introduced for lightly-loaded structures where settlement may occur. Piling and ground beams are the most expensive choice of foundation and are used where there is bad ground, or heavy loads need to be transmitted.

Basements are sometimes constructed on sloping sites in order to reduce unnecessary filling. It is generally a cheaper alternative to excavate and cart away rather than to provide hardcore bulk filling. Such basement areas can then be used for purposes such as car parking. Basements are also sometimes provided to tall buildings to reduce the pressure on the subsoil below the foundations, or to act as a counterbalance to the superstructure. It should be remembered, however, that the problems of waterproofing (such as tanking) can be expensive.

Quantity surveyors may be requested to compare the alternative costs of foundations where a choice is available. They may be also asked about the cost implications of adjusting the levels of the ground floor, providing more or less filling or providing some form of split-level construction on steeply-sloping sites.

The cost of foundations will be expressed in terms of cost per m^2 of the gross internal floor area. This cost will vary both for the size of the building and also in relationship to the number of storeys.

Size

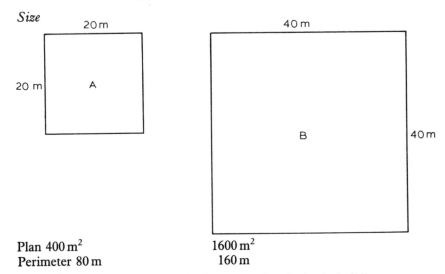

Plan 400 m^2 1600 m^2
Perimeter 80 m   160 m

Assuming a similar method of construction in both buildings, we can calculate their costs accordingly.

		A		B
Ground slab	400 m^2 @ £15	6000	1600 m^2 @ £15	24 000
Foundation	80 m @ £60	4800	160 m @ £60	9600
		£10 800		£33 600

Costs per m^2 GIFA   = £27   = £21

This reduction in plan B is due largely to its lower wall-to-floor ratio.

Number of storeys

The ground floor slab will have a constant unit rate – regardless of the number of storeys – assuming the method of construction does not change. This cost is expressed in terms of per square metre of gross internal floor area; therefore, the more upper floors that are introduced the lower will be its relative cost. In building A, assuming a single-storey construction, the cost per m^2 GIFA equals £15.00. If building A was two storeys then this comparable rate would reduce to £7.50 and for three storeys £5.00. The overall cost, it should be noted, will not change. This information can be tabulated as follows:

No. of storeys	Ground floor slab cost ratio	Rate per m^2	Rate per m^2 GIFA
1	1.00	15.00	15.00
2	0.50	15.00	7.50
3	0.33	15.00	5.00
4	0.25	15.00	3.75
5	0.20	15.00	3.00

Whilst traditional strip foundations will be satisfactory up to four or five storeys, the method of construction beyond these will need to change to something more substantial. Reinforced concrete column bases and attached ground beams may be suitable up to nine or ten storeys, but beyond that little choice is available other than to select one of the alternative types of piling systems. Different systems of piling have their own advantages, and specialist piling companies are usually ready to offer their advice in connection with early cost investigations.

Substructure costs (per m^2 GIFA) should therefore reduce up to five storeys even after allowing for some increase in the costs of the wall foundations. There will then be some increase in this cost to account for the more expensive foundation construction as the number of storeys increase. This will again taper off at about nine storeys when a sudden increase in cost should be expected to allow for one of the various types of piling.

Foundation cost

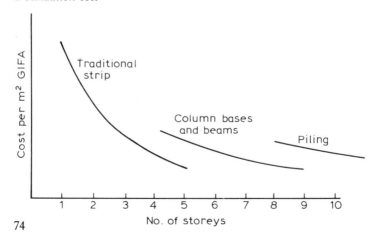

Illustrate with examples how the grouping of buildings can affect the initial building cost.

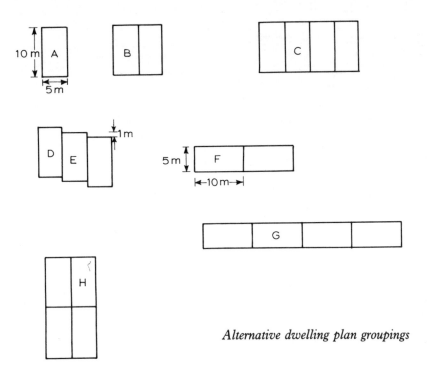

Alternative dwelling plan groupings

The above plans represent dwellings equal in area, heights and materials used. It must also be assumed at this stage that the layout of each dwelling is identical and is unaffected because of a change in orientation. Plan H, although it is the forbidden 'back to back' design, has been introduced for comparison purposes only. Some adjustments to the layout and the positions of windows would be necessary but for these examples they have been ignored, and the walling is measured gross.

By considering the above plans, the differences in costs which occur because of changes in grouping can be examined more closely. Changes in costs that might be expected by building several dwellings on a single site have not been considered. A change in building costs results largely because of a change in the external wall perimeter, with the floor area remaining constant. However, the wall-to-floor ratio of each dwelling does not change, but costs vary because of the sharing in costs of the party walls between dwellings. The amount of wall finishing inside of each dwelling will therefore remain unchanged.

House plan B, for example, has 20 m of external wall and 10 m of party wall. For comparative purposes, therefore, half of the party wall would be used in the cost comparison, i.e. 5 m. House plan F, which is a broad-fronted version of the same dwelling type and layout, has an external wall length of

75

25 m but an equivalent party wall length of 2.5 m. The staggered end of terrace dwelling D has lengths of 21 m and 4.5 respectively. These data are summarised in the table below.

Perimeters and areas of walling

| Plan | External wall | | Party wall allowance | |
	Perimeter	Area	Length	Area
A	30.00	150 m²	–	–
B	20.00	100 m²	5.00	25 m²
C	10.00	50 m²	10.00	50 m²
D	21.00	105 m²	4.50	22.50 m²
E	12.00	60 m²	9.00	45 m²
F	25.00	125 m²	2.50	12.50 m²
G	20.00	100 m²	5.00	25 m²
H	15.00	75 m²	7.50	37.50 m²

The areas have been calculated on the assumption of flat-roofed construction with an overall building height of 5 m. The cost influence on the walling of pitched roofs with gables would depend upon the pitch and the span direction of the structural timbers. The above, however, provides the general cost implications of these schemes. If the costs of external walling (measured over all openings) is calculated as £28 per square metre and that for the internal party walling as £20, then the cost implications on the walling due to different groupings of buildings can be shown as follows.

Walling costs per plan type

Plan	Costs of external walls £	Costs of internal walls £	Total cost £
A	4200	–	4200
B	2800	500	3300
C	1400	1000	2400
D	2940	450	3390
E	1680	900	2580
F	3500	250	3750
G	2800	500	3300
H	2100	750	2850

This shows quite clearly that type A (the detached version) will be the most expensive in walling costs. The above items represent the major cost differences, therefore this also implies that type A will be the most expensive overall. The most cost-effective grouping is that of intermediate terraced dwelling type C, and with local authority housing in mind, this is the most common type in practice.

Examining these costs for a group of four houses in the manner indicated, we arrive at the following appropriate costs of external walling and internal party walling.

Walling costs per grouping type

Block	Grouping	Total cost £	Average cost per dwelling in the group £
A	4 type A	16 800	4200
B	4 type B	13 200	3300
C	2 type B 2 type C	11 400	2850
D	2 type D 2 type E	11 940	2985
F	4 type F	15 000	3750
G	2 type F 2 type G	14 200	3550
H	4 type H	11 400	2850

This shows that the narrow-fronted grouping (plan C) is the most cost-efficient, and further savings can be achieved where the number of dwellings in the terrace is increased. Obviously, for aesthetic and other considerations it is not desirable to develop a site using this type of grouping alone, and factors other than cost will then need to be examined.

The type of grouping will also affect sections other than external walls. For example, in practice there could be a different layout plan between plans G and C, to account for the differences in orientation. There is also likely to be a difference in the roof costs between these two types because the spans are different, resulting in a variation in the sizes of the structural members. The areas of roof covering, however, will remain unchanged. There may also be a difference in the costs of upper floors for this same reason.

In very broad terms, this cost study could show that the semi-detached or end-terraced version was approximately 6 per cent more expensive overall than a middle-terraced version (ignoring land charges and fees). The detached type would show itself to be 12 per cent more expensive than this cheapest alternative.

Discuss how a reduction in the storey height of a multi-storey office building will affect the elemental construction costs.

It may be suggested, for example, that a reduction in the storey height from 3.20 m to 2.80 might be envisaged. The ensuing discussion or calculation, however, will incorporate guidelines regardless of the size of the reduction. The methods and materials of construction are not assumed to vary unless this change in design particularly affects the process or systems used. A reinforced concrete framed structure with brick infill, concrete floors, standard finishings (for owner occupation) and modern engineering services are the assumptions made in respect of the specification.

Some of the elements would remain unaffected by this design change in respect of the storey height. These would include the upper floors, roof, floor finishes, fittings and sanitary appliances. The elements to be examined include only those associated with the building and do not include external works or drainage, which should remain unaffected.

It is unlikely at the cost planning stage that any reduction would be made to the element substructure. The overall height, using my assumptions, will be reduced by approximately 12 per cent, and this may allow for a less expensive foundation design. As well as reducing the weight of the building, some examination of the site and soil conditions would also be necessary.

By reducing the overall height of the building, the frame will be cheaper in two respects: first, the actual savings achieved due to the shorter lengths of the columns required, and secondly the possible savings expected because of an overall reduction in the load on the remaining columns. Larger-sized columns would be required on the lower floors and their cross-sectional area could possibly be reduced.

The staircase element would show some saving because of a reduction in the number of treads and risers required. A straight proportionate reduction could not be made to the staircase element because it is likely that some landings would be included within its overall element cost.

The external wall element could also not be recalculated by using a direct proportion of the alternative storey heights. Adjustments may need to take into account the overall building heights of the two office blocks. It might also be assumed that the reduction in the storey heights could be fully compensated for within the brick infill construction. If this was the case then the element of windows and external doors might remain unaffected. This would largely depend upon the architect's decision regarding the revised elevations together with the amount of natural light required for the office building.

The areas of the internal walls and partitions and the wall finishes will be largely reduced in the same proportion as the storey heights. If, however, an expensive wall finish such as tiling were envisaged up to a height of, say, 2.0 m in some of the rooms then this calculation would become invalid, and the costs of a less expensive finish would need to be reduced when assessing any changes.

It is unlikely that any change in the total cost of the element internal doors would be necessary, unless the use of storey height frames had been envisaged. It might, however, be considered a little unusual to use this method of construction for heights of 3.20 m.

The ceiling finishes element would remain unchanged if the specification was assumed to be the same. A storey height of 2.80 m might be assumed to be a minimum for office construction, so that any finish used might be applied directly to the soffit of the concrete suspended floors. With a storey height of 3.20 m, more usual in office construction, suspended ceilings might have been incorporated within the specification. The height reduction could therefore result in a considerable saving, but some attention would possibly need to be paid to the rerouting of the services and the costs associated with alternative ductwork, that otherwise may have been hidden in the ceiling void.

The costs of the disposal installation might include waste pipes to the sanitary fittings, soil and ventilating pipes, refuse chutes, incinerators, etc. Some reduction in cost might be expected because of the shorter lengths of pipework due to the reduced storey height. The overall cost reduction, however, would be marginal and no adjustment would probably be made to the analysis. The cost effects of a reduced storey height on the elements water installations, space heating and electrical installations would be examined in a similar way. There are some savings in cost, and possibly in an office block with a large number of storeys some adjustments to a cost plan might be made. This same argument would be used for the lift installation element. The costs of this element would include the lift compartment, access doors to each floor, the lift motor, the lift motor room and the builders' work. None of these items will have a significant cost difference to that envisaged in the original analysis.

A boiler with a reduced output may be considered because the total volume of air to be treated is less on account of the lower storey height. A reduction in the element cost for the heat source might therefore be made. Using this same argument, a reduction in the efficiency of any air-conditioning plant could be made, and this might result in a less expensive plant being selected. The most critical factor to consider here is the resiting of ducts and ventilators due to a possible loss of the ceiling space that might have been considered useful for their position in the building.

The preliminaries element might have been separately analysed in which case it may remain unchanged, although some reduction in the overall contract period could be expected. If, however, the costs of this element have been added as a percentage to the construction costs, which is more likely, then this would be revised in the same proportion as the reduction in the total costs of the elements described above.

Overall there will be a reduction in both the total cost of the scheme and, because the floor area will remain the same, in the cost per square metre of gross internal floor area. It is unlikely that any element will show an increase in cost, but because some of the elements remain unchanged, and the fact that some of these are of major cost significance, a reduction considerably below 12 per cent of the original analysis would be expected.

9 Costs in use

Your client, a restaurant proprietor, has asked your advice on floor finishes for a new restaurant which he is building. He estimates the economic life of the restaurant at 30 years and has told you to assume a 5 per cent discount rate.

There are two floor finishes under consideration:

(1) Type A having a life of 15 years, an initial cost of £20 000, nil annual maintenance cost and cleaning costs of £750 per annum.
(2) Type B having a life of 30 years and having annual maintenance costs of £250 and cleaning costs of £750 per annum.

(a) Advise your client how much could be spent initially on Type B floor finish so that the overall costs of Type A and Type B flooring are the same.
(b) List any factors, other than those given above, which should be taken into account before deciding on which floor finish should be adopted.

(a) This part of the question is essentially a discounted cash flow calculation. The student needs to be able to convert cash flows at different periods of time into a common time-scale. The time-scales selected are usually either on the basis of a present value, annual equivalent sum or future amount. In this particular question an initial cost is required for Type B floor finish and therefore the question determines the selection of the present value approach. Assumptions sometimes need to be made about expected life and the discount rate to be selected. In this question they are given; where they are not, current values should be used. Two tables only need to be used. (1) 'The present value of £1'. This is the amount which must be invested now in order to accumulate to £1 at compound interest. (2) 'The present value of £1 per annum'. This is the amount which must be invested now in order to accumulate to £1 per annum at compound interest.

The calculations can be set down as follows:

Economic life 30 years	*Discount rate 5 per cent*
Type A	*Present value (£)*
Initial cost £20 000	£20 000
Maintenance Nil	–
Cleaning £750 p.a. × 15.3725	11 529
Replacement £20 000 yr 15 × 0.481017	9620
Present value	£41 149

The above calculation converts all present and future sums to present values. £20 000 is a present value. Cleaning costs are £750 per annum, therefore the table 'Present value of £1 per annum' is used. The number of years is 30 and the discount rate indicated is 5 per cent. Because the expected life of floor finish A is only 15 years, renewal is required at year 15. The appropriate value from the 'present value of £1' table is therefore selected. Maintenance costs are treated in exactly the same way as cleaning costs.

A similar approach is then applied to the Type B floor finish. The initial cost is the figure to be calculated and this is the remainder of the sum up to £40 691.

Type B	Present value (£)
Initial cost	£25 777
Maintenance £250 p.a. × 15.3725	£ 3843
Cleaning £750 p.a. × 15.3725	£11 529
Replacement	Nil
	£41 149

Because floor finish B is to have an expected life of 30 years, no replacement costs need to be considered. £25 777 is the answer to part (a).

(b)(i) Prestige.

(ii) As well as being more durable, expensive construction is generally more pleasant to look at.

(iii) Replacement or repairs may be inconvenient.

(iv) Replacement or repairs may be difficult and therefore expensive.

(v) The saving of money on a specific item may involve costs out of all proportion to the saving.

(vi) Obsolescence may not be a factor to be considered.

(vii) The client may be concerned with spending more initially in order to reduce running costs.

Describe the alternative methods that can be used for investment appraisal, indicating their advantages and disadvantages.

Discounting methods

(1) The net present value (NPV). In order to determine the NPV of a proposed investment, the forecast net-of-tax cash flows are simply discounted to the tune of the initial capital outlay (at a rate chosen to reflect the company's cost of capital) and the value of the initial capital outlay subtracted. The company's cost of capital is generally set at a level which would give the shareholders a rate of return at least equal to what they could obtain outside the company. The discounting technique can be readily adapted to take account of real-life complications such as cash flows arising in the middle of a year, investment grants, capital allowances, inflation, and delays in corporation tax payments. With the help of appropriate tables, the volume of calculation and analysis resulting from these complications is not nearly as weighty as might be supposed.

(2) Internal rate of return (IRR). This is the most common discounting method of investment appraisal. It can be defined as that rate of interest which, when used to discount the net of tax cash flows of a proposed investment, reduces the NPV of the project to zero. This discount rate can be found by trial and error: if a negative NPV results, the rate chosen is too high; if a positive NPV is obtained, the rate is too low. Although it appears to involve a large number of calculations, in practice it should never be

necessary to carry out more than two trial discounts, the true IRR then being determined by interpolation. The IRR depicts the annual rate of return on the capital outstanding on the investment. Thus, in common with the NPV method, the IRR will generally be higher if the bulk of the cash flows are received earlier rather than later in the life of the project, reflecting the fact that more capital will have been recovered in the first years of the project so that the flows remaining represent a higher rate of return.

(3) Necessity/postponability. This criterion is essentially a negative one. The rationale is that the more postponable an investment is, the less attractive it appears and so the basis of investment decision making is the urgency of requirements. Thus, if Project A was one which could only be carried out now and could not be initiated at a later date, it would be chosen in favour of a project which could be undertaken in the future.

Conventional methods

(1) *Pay-back method.* This is the crudest form of investment criterion, but nevertheless the most widely used. It is defined as the period it takes for an investment to generate sufficient incremental cash to recover its initial capital outlay in full. A cut-off point can be chosen, beyond which the project will be rejected if the investment has not been paid off. The payback method appears attractive because it is extremely simple to apply. Since the payback method takes cash receipts into account, it helps to assess a company's future cash flow (particularly advantageous in times of liquidity crisis). However, it fails to measure long-term profitability since it takes no account of cash flows beyond the payback period. It is therefore difficult to make comparisons between projects using this criterion. The technique also falls short in its application within the payback period, since no account is taken of the timing of the cash flows during that period. The use of the method is sometimes justified by claiming that it is a 'dynamic' criterion since projects are adopted only if they are paid off quickly, but this argument does not allow for the fact that highly profitable investments do not necessarily pay off in the initial years although large gains may be reaped later.

(2) *Average rate of return method.* The average rate of return is the ratio of profit (net of depreciation) to capital. The first decision that must be made is how to define profit and capital. Profit can be taken as either gross of tax or net of tax, but since businesses are mostly interested in their post-tax position, net profit is a more useful yardstick. However, net profit can be either that which is made in the first year, or the average of what is made over the entire lifetime of the project. Similarly, capital can be taken as either the initial sum invested or as a form of average over the time of all the capital outlays over the life of the project. This method takes no account of the incidence of cash flows so that projects with the same capital costs, expected length of life and total profitability would be ranked as equally acceptable. The method can, however, be extended by calculating the net average yield. This is done by subtracting the stream of cash outlays from the stream of cash benefits and expressing the answer as a percentage of the initial outlay.

(3) *Optimal investment criterion.* Although some of the conventional methods of investment appraisal provide a useful measure of the vulnerability of investment proposals to risk and liquidity constraints, for gauging the profitability of project they are extremely inferior to the discounting methods because of their failure to recognise that money has a true value. There are

occasions when IRR is meaningless. If, for example, a particular project involves heavy net capital outlays towards the end of its life, the IRR could be nonsensical. When appraising independent projects, where the only decision to be made is whether to accept the project or not, then both the NPV method and the IRR method will give the same answer. However, when trying to decide which is the most profitable of two mutually exclusive projects, the two methods can give very different answers. The risks associated with a project are largely dependent on the quantity of capital involved and the length of the project. By showing a rate per unit of capital per unit of time of the project, the IRR can show the margin over the cost of capital that is being obtained in return for any risk taken.

Conventional methods of dealing with risk, such as sensitivity analysis, probability analysis and game theory, can be used in conjunction with discounting techniques.

In considering the heating system for a proposed new building, the heating engineer has provided details of two systems.

Boiler	*System A*	*System B*
Initial cost	£120 000	£140 000
Overhaul	£20 000 (5-yearly)	£10 000 (3-yearly)
Major replacement	£40 000 (15th year)	£5000 (12th year)
Life of boiler	30 years	40 years
Heat transfer		
Units and pipework		
Initial cost	£42 000	£42 000
Repairs	£2000 p.a.	£2000 p.a.
Fuel	£15 000 p.a.	£14 000 p.a.
Staff costs	£12 000 p.a.	£8000 p.a.

The building is to be used for 30 years by a Charitable Trust, which pays no tax and which has a cost of capital of 5 per cent net of inflation.

Fully evaluate the two options.

Note to candidates: this question follows a very similar pattern to a previous example. The procedure is to reduce all present and future payments into a common time-scale. The discounting rate has been given in the question but where this was left to the candidates' discretion a rate similar to current interest rates might be adopted.

Although the project is a proposed new building that might be expected to have a life of at least 60 years, the building will only be occupied by the present client for 30 years. The costs to the charitable trust will, therefore, extend for this period only. The problems of selling the building after 30 years without a suitable heating system would be ignored, and although System B would still have a useful life of a further ten years, a new client might wish to replace the system with a new one at this time. An overhaul of both boiler systems is required at periodic intervals; System A 5 years and System B 3 years. Major overhaul of the boilers is also required at years 15 and 12 respectively.

As well as being less expensive, System A initially requires fewer shut-down periods, which is more convenient. However, the amount to be spent on System A for repairs and replacement is considerably in excess of that for System B, indicating more extensive work probably with a longer shut-down period. Any repairs to the structure caused by these maintenance problems are assumed to be included in the appropriate figures. It is further assumed that when a major replacement of the boiler occurs, no overhaul is necessary. Therefore with System A there will be no overhual in year 15. Because the building's life, as far as the Charitable Trust is concerned, is only 30 years, overhaul and replacement are not necessary in year 30. The same approach would apply to System B. However, it can be seen in System B that the major replacement is less than the overhaul. It must be assumed in this case that shorter periods of overhaul prevent a large major replacement in years 12 and 24. The 40-year expected life of the boiler in System B is largely irrelevant, because it exceeds the building's expected usage of 30 years.

The calculations can be set out as follows:
Both systems 30-year life 5 per cent discount rate.

System A

Boiler

Initial cost		=	120 000

Overhaul £20 000/5 years

Year 5	0.783526		
Year 10	0.613913		
Year 15	Replace		
Year 20	0.376889		
Year 25	0.295303		
Year 30	Required for 30 years only		
	$\overline{2.069631} \times £20\,000$	=	41 393

Major replacement year 15
$£40\,000 \times 0.481017$ = 19 241

Heat transfer

Initial cost		=	42 000
Repairs	2000 p.a.		
Fuel	15 000 p.a.		
Staff	12 000 p.a.		
	$\overline{£29\,000} \times 15.3725$	=	445 803
			£668 437

The above figures have each been converted to net present values for comparative purposes. The discount rates for the overhaul and replacement have been obtained from the present value of £1 table, and the repairs, fuel and staff costs being annual sums from the present value of £1 per annum table.

System B

Boiler

Initial cost	=	140 000

Overhaul £10 000/3 years

Year 3	0.863838
Year 6	0.746215
Year 9	0.644609
Year 12	Replace
Year 15	0.481017
Year 18	0.415521
Year 21	0.358942
Year 24	Replace
Year 27	0.267848
Year 30	Required for 30 years only

$$\overline{3.777990} \times £10\,000 \qquad = \qquad 37\,780$$

Major replacement

Year 12	0.556837
Year 24	0.310068

$$\overline{0.866905} \times £5000 \qquad = \qquad 4335$$

Heat transfer

Initial cost	=	42 000

Repairs   2000 p.a.
Fuel   14 000 p.a.
Staff   8000 p.a.

$$\overline{24\,000} \times 15.3725 \qquad = \quad 368\,940$$
$$\text{NPV} \quad £593\,055$$

Each of these sums can be expressed and compared as annual equivalents.

$$AE = \frac{NPV}{\text{Present value of £1 per annum}}$$

$$A = \frac{668\,437}{15.3725} \qquad £43\,483$$

$$B = \frac{59\,055}{15.3725} \qquad £38\,579$$

Advice to the Trust would consider the following:

(1) System A has the lower initial cost.
(2) System B has an overall cost advantage.
(3) System B is likely to be less affected by inflationary tendencies, e.g. annual cost on System B £24 000 and on System A £29 000. System A is also more expensive on overhauls and replacement costs.
(4) If the initial capital cost is available System B is the more economic proposition.

An office complex of 10 000 m² gross floor area and let to a number of tenants at rents of £50 per square metre per annum is owned by an investment company.

The complex is heated by means of pipework from a district heating distribution in the road. The method avoids the necessity for a boiler plant in the complex but the charge made by the heat distribution company, currently £75 000 per annum, has been continually rising. Your client, the investment company, is considering providing its own boiler plant and discontinuing with the street supply. The proposal would result in a reduction of floor space of 5 per cent.

Advise the client on the maximum allowable cost of the boiler plant for the proposal to be economically viable, and discuss fully any other factors that should be brought to your client's attention.

The answer to this question depends very much upon the assumptions to be made. Answers different from the one given should be expected. It is a good question and is very practically biased.

Rents

The office complex has a 10 000 m² gross (internal) floor area. It should be remembered that rents are usually calculated on the lettable floor area. A 10–15 per cent reduction from the above area will need to be made before calculating the annual rental. At this stage any increases in the rental sum (to cover inflation) can be ignored and may anyway only balance future expenditure.

10 000 m² gross floor area × 90 per cent × £50 = £450 000 p.a.

The proposal to change the method of heating from a district heating distribution to one from its own boiler supply, would either reduce the floor area (overall) or necessitate the building of a boiler house. It is assumed that space is not available on site for a boiler house, so the boiler plant must be sited somewhere within the building. The amount of space required would depend upon the size of the plant and also the existing arrangement within the office building. If a 5 per cent reduction in the floor area could be achieved this would result in a loss of rent per annum of:

£450 000 × 5 per cent = £22 500

It is further assumed that any charges for heating will be borne separately and directly by the office clients, and that this would not affect the rental charges.

District heating costs

The heat distribution company currently charge £75 000 per annum. It must be assumed that the office block has been occupied for some time, and that initially it was either a viable economic form of heating or a condition imposed by the original developers of the site. It is assumed, therefore, that a further 30 years useful life could be expected, and that the current rate of capital is 10 per cent.

Annual charge for heating		£75 000
Less loss of rent		£22 500
Annaul comparative cost	=	£52 500

The present value of this sum over an expected life of a further 30 years can be calculated as:

£52 500 × 9.427 (10 per cent from tables at 30 years) = £494 918

Costs of alternative heating system

This is the total sum of money the client has available to convert from district heating and for fuel and repairs throughout this period. It would have to allow for:

(1) The cost of the boiler plant.
(2) The use of the existing distribution and heat exchange equipment would remain unchanged.
(3) The costs of the alterations to accommodate a boiler room. Additional costs may also be involved in providing adequate insulation and fire protection, particularly to those offices near the plant room.
(4) The running costs of the boiler.
(5) The maintenance of this equipment.
(6) The costs of renewing this equipment. If it is assumed that the boiler plant will only provide a 30-year useful life, any costs associated with this item can be ignored.

The following is an attempt to quantify the foregoing information:

(1) The present value cost of any alterations both for the plant room and to provide suitable insulation. 5 per cent 10 000 m² × £150 (assumed cost of alterations per square metre) = £75 000

(2) Running costs. This can be calculated on the basis of a rate per square metre of lettable floor area per annum. It will, of course, have to be discounted to a net present value. 10 000 m² × 90 per cent (lettable) × 95 per cent (plant room) × 9.427 (discount rate 10 per cent for 30 years) × £2.50 (assumed rate for heating per m²) = £201 502

(3) Maintenance costs. Allow 10 per cent of running costs = £20 150

(4) The maximum allowable sum for the boiler and its associated plant and equipment = £198 266

£494 918

The total cost appraisal technique, whilst excellent in theory, has considerable problems in practice. Discuss.

Construction projects were once almost entirely evaluated upon their initial construction costs alone. No attempt was made to try to estimate the recurring costs in use associated with the maintenance or repair of the fabric or the costs attributed to the operation of engineering services. The choice of an economic solution involved only the comparison of possible tender sums. In more recent times it has been recognised that by increasing spending marginally at the time of construction, savings can be achieved, and in some cases recovered fairly quickly, on costs in use. The total cost appraisal technique seeks to evaluate alternative design solutions not solely on the basis of initial construction costs, but by combining these with the costs in use in order to select the optimum solution. The costs occur at different periods of time, therefore, some method of discounting future costs needs to be employed. This makes an investment appraisal technique necessary, and an immediate problem arises in that the alternative methods available do not always achieve the same solution.

The major difficulties associated with the use of this technique in practice can be summarised as follows:

(1) There is a scarcity of reliable and accurate historical cost information suitable for costs-in-use calculations. Only in more recent times has anyone considered it useful to collect and analyse maintenance cost information. The Building Maintenance Cost Information Service, a forerunner in this respect, was established for this purpose. The Property Services Agency has also undertaken some studies on the maintenance of their Crown Offices. Apart from these sources, little information is available on the costs of cleaning, heating, repairs, etc. in buildings.

(2) There are the problems associated with accurately predicting the maintenance and running costs of different materials, processes and systems. Even when data are available, they are often so variable as to be virtually useless. Wide variations in maintenance costs can be expected for apparently similar situations. The quantity surveyor may have to rely upon his own knowledge or experience of a material or component or on the manufacturer's assessment, particularly for new products. Daily use, climate, general care and trends in fashion will influence the maintenance costs. Even where data are available on the useful economic life of a constructional process, in practice this period is often considerably extended.

(3) The total cost appraisal techniques generally require all payments to be related to a common basis for comparison purposes. The initial costs of construction, the annual running costs of engineering services and the periodic costs of building maintenance all need to be evaluated in this way. This calls for a knowledge of discounted cash flow techniques incorporating the use of valuation formulae.

(4) The selection of suitable interest rates for calculations of 60 years or more is very difficult. When carrying out costs-in-use calculations, it is necessary to discount future sums of expenditure or income. In order to do these calculations, appropriate interest rates need to be selected. Although different rates could be chosen, for simplicity and without a loss of accuracy,

a single rate is used for the full lifetime of the building. It is not possible to predict with any degree of certainty interest rates that might prevail in five years time, let alone the much longer periods of time into the future that are required in these calculations.

(5) Changes in taxation rates and policies of allowances will vary over the life of a building. Taxation has an influence on building maintenance costs, and therefore cannot be ignored in the calculation. The rules regarding Value Added Tax are also unlikely to remain the same throughout a building's life. Government currently awards grants, for example, for house improvement and for enticing industry to certain areas. These will have a bearing on any calculation and are subject to regular review.

(6) The effects of inflation do not affect all costs in a uniform manner. Increases in the costs of two alternative systems are unlikely to run parallel. The effect of unequal inflation is to distort the results of a costs-in-use calculation. This can, in extreme circumstances, eventually show the reverse of what was actually calculated as an optimum scheme.

(7) Initial funds may not be available to choose the appropriate scheme, and interest rates may be so high as to make borrowing for such prohibitive. This might suggest that a client is satisfied on the best scheme he should adopt, but because of the large sums of money required initially, he is unable to take this course of action.

(8) How the building will be disposed of on completion will determine the costs to be spent initially. If the building is for owner occupation, it may be important to minimise the costs incurred during its use. If it is to be let, the building owner will primarily be concerned with those costs in use for which he is responsible. If the building is to be sold, the owner will only be concerned with spending funds initially that are going to make it an attractive proposition for a possible buyer.

Perhaps, after examining the above difficulties associated with total cost appraisal, the problems might seem to be too great for its useful application in practice. But there are two points in its favour. First, it is always better to have an objective as well as a subjective viewpoint. It is therefore preferable to provide some calculation wherever this is possible. Secondly, costs included for some expenditure in the distant future will be of a lesser magnitude after discounting, and therefore their effect on the calculation is of much less importance.

Discuss the effects of rising energy costs on (1) total annual premises costs; (2) the design of buildings; (3) the availability of energy resources.

(1) In order the discuss the effects of rising energy costs on annual premises costs we need to define the contents of the latter. The Building Maintenance Cost Information Service (BMCIS) have prepared a standard format of how such costs should be analysed irrespective of the type of building. This allows for easy comparison between different building types. The format is similar to a traditional cost analysis but includes elements as follows:

(a) Decoration.
(b) Fabric – maintenance and repairs of the structure and finishings.
(c) Services – maintenance and repairs to all types of engineering services.
(d) Cleaning.
(e) Utilities — energy supply, water and sewage treatment.
(f) Administrative costs – such as security and property management.
(g) Overheads – insurance and rates.
(h) External works – which includes gardening.

In addition, there is provision on the form for improvements and adaptations which may have been carried out during the year. The intention is to complete the analysis on an annual basis.

An increase in energy costs, whilst affecting element (e) above the most seriously, will also have a spin-off effect indirectly affecting each of the other elements. For example, an increase in the costs of energy to an increase in the costs of energy to an industry manufacturing paints will cause their prices charged for their commodities to rise, and this will then be reflected in element (a) above.

The total annual premises costs will also be influenced by the purpose for which the building is used. An industry using vast quantities of energy for a manufacturing process will be much more affected in real terms than, say, an office which may use energy supplies only for heating and lighting. This will still be the case after taking any subsidies into account. For example, assuming that the other elemental costs remain the same and energy represents 50 per cent of the total annual premises costs on building X but only 20 per cent on building Y. A 15 per cent rise in energy costs will cause the total premises costs in A to rise by 7.5 per cent but in B by only 2.25 per cent. Building A therefore will experience both a greater rise in real terms and also as a percentage than building B.

The distribution of costs between these elements will also be influenced by the age of the building. During the building's early life, decoration, maintenance and repairs are likely to be much smaller proportions than when the building has been in use for a number of years. This view is supported by a study of Crown Office Buildings carried out by the Department of the Environment.

The total annual premises costs for private domestic buildings will be severely affected by rises in the costs of energy. Although their actual increases will be substantially smaller than an industry's, the overall

90

percentage rise can be much larger. The reason for this is that their energy costs will be the highest sum largely because many of the maintenance, repair and cleaning costs will be carried out on an ownership basis and therefore excluded from the analysis.

(2) Building design was once used to provide a scheme free from almost any restraints. When cost became an important factor to consider, great stress was laid upon initial value for money. In more recent times some emphasis has been placed upon achieving the best solution taking into account not just initial building costs but also the costs in use. One of the reasons for this change in emphasis has been the rising energy costs.

The design of buildings now almost always incorporates some form of energy-saving measures. These may include improved thermal insulation to roofs, walls and windows, and some of these can in the short term be financed out of future savings in energy costs. Greater emphasis is also placed upon achieving solar gains by positioning the aspect of the building and by the introduction of solar heating panels. Provision has also been made for greater efficiency of heating systems by installing improved control technology.

In order to enforce an energy-saving programme, all new construction works must now comply with more stringent building regulations. These have as one of their aims the reduction of heat loss from buildings. Designers are sometimes prepared to exceed these regulations in order to provide improved thermal conditions. Eventually we may find provision in cost yardsticks to allow for increased thermal construction or taxation allowances to encourage these aspects in design.

Rising energy costs may also have the effect of eliminating those building materials which are expensive in energy cost to manufacture. New materials may therefore be developed based upon a low-energy technology.

It has long been recognised that complex plan shapes or excessive storey heights are expensive both in their initial construction cost and also in heat losses for an equivalent floor space area. Building shape has become more cost-important in recent years, and storey heights in most buildings now are probably the minimum that could be expected. Rising energy costs may therefore tend to bring more buildings within these parameters.

(3) Worldwide energy demand is expected to continue to grow for the foreseeable future. Increases in the costs of energy will possibly assist people to change their lifelong habits and, at least in the short term, reduce consumption and thereby help to conserve resources. Traditionally we have relied upon the fossil fuels of coal, oil and gas, and to a small extent hydro-electric schemes. Both gas and oil supplies will be exhausted early in the next century, and it seems unlikely that high cost alone, without some form of physical rationing, will be able to extend their lives for many more years. Greatly increased dependence on nuclear energy, with all its political ramifications, seems inescapable.

Other options for energy resources will therefore have to be investigated. Some of the currently expensive alternatives will become cost-effective due to rising costs of traditional energy resources. These may include: greater attention to coal utilisation; high priorities to North Sea gas and oil; safe nuclear technology; alternative sources such as solar, wind, wave, waste materials, etc; improving the efficiency of energy-using equipment and a major effort on energy saving such as the 'Save-it' campaign.

A church council is considering two alternative proposals to accommodate an increasing congregation. Two schemes exist:

(1) Extension of the existing building with modifications to the old building.
(2) Demolition and rebuilding.

The following are the financial implications.

Scheme 1

	£
Proposed extension, including fees	120 000
Repairs and modifications	80 000
Major repairs every 15 years	15 000
General maintenance per annum	2000
Redecoration every eight years	10 000
Heating per annum	1800
Lighting and cleaning per annum	1000
Insurances per annum	900

Scheme 2

	£
Demolition, sale of materials etc.	−30 000
Building and fees	350 000
General maintenance per annum	500
Redecoration every 10 years	9000
Heating per annum	900
Lighting and cleaning per annum	800
Insurances per annum	750

Evaluate the above proposals, suggesting other factors that may need to be considered.

It is assumed for comparative purposes that both projects will have an equal life, and in this example it is assumed to be 60 years. This may be a false opinion concerning scheme 1, since the age of the existing building is not known. This may indicate that larger sums of money at some future date will need to be expended to reduce the obsolescence factor, although £80 000 has been allowed for possible modernisation now. It is also assumed that the existing building is suitable for, and capable of, extensive alterations. The discount rate selected would be that representing the current cost of capital.

Scheme 1 – Extension and internal modifications

	£
Extension and fees	120 000
Repairs/modifications	80 000

Major repairs every 15 years
Year	15	0.23939
Year	30	0.05731
Year	45	0.01372

0.31042 × £15 000	=	4654

Redecoration every eight years

	Year	8	0.46651
	Year	16	0.21763
	Year	24	0.10153
	Year	32	0.04736
	Year	40	0.02209
	Year	48	0.01031
	Year	56	0.00481

$$0.8724 \times £10\,000 \quad = \quad 8702$$

General maintenance 2000
Heating   1800
Lighting/cleaning   1000
Insurances   900

$$9.967 \times \overline{5700} \qquad = \qquad 56\,812$$

Present value of scheme 1   £270 170

Annual equivalent of scheme 1   £ 27 106

Scheme 2 – New building

			£
Demolition			30 000
Building and fees			350 000

Redecoration every 10 years

Year	10	0.38554
Year	20	0.14864
Year	30	0.05731
Year	40	0.02209
Year	50	0.00852

$$0.62210 \times £9000 \qquad = \qquad 5598$$

General maintenance 500
Heating   900
Lighting/cleaning   800
Insurances   750

$$9.967 \times \overline{2950} \qquad = \qquad 29\,403$$

Present value of scheme 2   £355 001

Annual equivalent of scheme 2   £35 618

The final totals are presented both on the basis of present values and annual equivalents. The annual equivalents are found by dividing the present value totals by the appropriate amount of the 'present value of £1 per annum', in this case for a 60-year period at 10 per cent. The major repairs every 15 years and the redecoration every eight years are discounted to their present values using the 'present value of £1 table'. This table is used since these are periodic sums. The remaining amounts are all of a regular annual nature. Although some will be paid at weekly intervals and others as a single yearly payment, no distinction has been made in the calculations to allow for this minor adjustment. All these sums are discounted using the 'present value of £1 per annum table'. The amounts for scheme 2 have been presented in a similar way.

On the basis of these data and the above calculations, the proposed extension with modifications to the existing building is the most economic solution. Interest rates would need to rise considerably to reverse this opinion. The following points, however, should also be borne in mind when advising the church council.

(1) The extension to the church could be carried out and completed before any of the modernisation work was commenced. This phased programme would then always allow some part of the church buildings to remain in use. This may be a further important factor in support of this scheme. A phased start to the whole project would also give the church authorities more time to arrange their finance.

(2) It is assumed that the proposed church will occupy the same site and location on the site. Demolition would therefore be a prerequisite to any new building project. The church council would, therefore, have to find alternative accommodation close by for a period of up to twelve months. During this period the church could find itself losing a part of the congregation and so alleviating the original problem.

(3) Planning and ecclesiastical restrictions may prohibit the demolition of the existing church, particularly if it were of special architectural interest.

(4) A new building should be more efficiently designed in terms of space and constructional details. Other important factors such as dual usage might also be considered. The refurbishment of the existing building has to be undertaken within the confines of the existing structure and this will place some limits on the design.

(5) Although the life of the existing building is to be extended by refurbishment, it may be found in practice that due to obsolescence and constructional weakness this will not be so.

(6) Some form of cost limit may be in force restricting the amount of funds available initially. An outdated comparison between the two competing proposals might therefore favour scheme 1 on the basis of initial building costs only.

A local authority is considering various forms of heating for a housing scheme of 800 dwellings. There are four alternatives under consideration:

(1) A district heating scheme with central boiler house, distribution mains and heat exchangers in individual dwellings providing warm air heating and hot water; or

(2) Electric underfloor heating and immersion hot water heaters in individual dwellings; or

(3) Gas-fired small bore central heating and hot water in individual dwellings; or

(4) Solid fuel back boiler heating two radiators and providing hot water and supplemented by electric panel radiators.

Estimates of the alternatives, including the cost of builder's work, have been prepared. Calculate and compare the present values and annual equivalents for the installation, repair and running costs of the four alternatives over a 60-year life. The present value should be shown as a total for the whole scheme and the annual equivalent for individual dwellings. Assume an interest rate of 10 per cent.

Comment on the factors other than cost which should be taken into consideration when deciding which alternative should be chosen.

	£
Alternative (1)	
Capital cost of boiler house and plant	150 000
Renewal of plant every 20 years	50 000
Capital cost of distribution mains	50 000
Heat exchanger (per dwelling)	40
Running costs (per dwelling per year)	50
Alternative (2)	£
Capital cost of electricity mains	30 000
Installation per dwelling	200
Renewal every 30 years (per dwelling)	150
Running costs (per dwelling per year)	150
Alternative (3)	£
Capital cost of gas mains	45 000
Installation per dwelling	500
Modernisation of installation after 40 years (per dwelling)	100
Running costs (per dwelling per year)	75
Alternative (4)	£
Installation per dwelling – including provision of fuel shed	250
Replacement of boiler every 25 years (per dwelling)	40
Replacement of radiators every 15 years	100
Running costs (per dwelling per year)	100

Note. All dwellings must be provided with gas and electricity and the Electricity Board has agreed to lay the electricity mains free of charge if alternative (b) is chosen and the Gas Board to lay the gas mains free of charge if alternative (c) is chosen. The meter reading charges are included in the running costs.

The basis of this question is to convert all present and future payments to a common time-scale in order to provide a realistic economic evaluation. The question requires the comparison to be made on both a present value and an annual equivalent basis. Each of the dwellings will have a 60-year economic life and sums are to be discounted at a rate of 10 per cent. If electric underfloor heating is selected, the capital cost of the electricity mains will be provided free of change. A similar concession is made by the Gas Board for the cost of gas mains should gas central heating be selected.

(1) District heating

Cost of boiler house and plant	=	£150 000
Renewal of plant every 20 years		
Year 20 × £50 000 × 0.1486	=	7430
Year 40 × £50 000 × 0.0221	=	1105
Distribution mains	=	50 000
Heat exchanger £40 per dwelling × 800 dwellings	=	32 000
Running cost per dwelling £50 × 800 dwellings × 9.967	=	398 680
Cost of mains electricity	=	30 000
Cost of mains gas	=	45 000
Present value cost of district heating scheme	=	£714 215

The initial costs for the boiler house and plant, distribution mains, heat exchangers and incoming mains for gas and electricity are included in the calculations in the form given because they are present value sums. The cost of the heat exchanger must, of course, be multiplied by the number of dwellings. Renewal of the plant is required every 20 years, but as the economic life is stated as 60 years no renewal will be necessary in year 60. These amounts must be discounted by using the 'present value of £1 table' to convert them to present-value sums. The running costs are stated as £50 per annum per dwelling. This sum must be discounted to a present-value sum by using the 'present value of £1 per annum table'. Unlike the renewal of the plant, which is a periodic payment, the running costs are a regular annual payment and this is the reason for using the different tables.

The present value calculated as £714 215 can easily and quickly be converted to an annual equivalent, by dividing this sum by the present value of £1 per annum for 60 years at 10 per cent.

$$\frac{£714\,215}{9.967} = £71\,657$$

The annual equivalent is required for the individual dwellings, therefore, this amount must be divided by the number of dwellings.

$$\frac{£71\,657}{800 \text{ dwellings}} = £89.57$$

A similar process is then used to calculate the appropriate amounts for the other alternative systems, remembering to consider separately, initial, periodic and annual payments.

(2) Electric underfloor heating

Installation £200 per dwelling		
£200 × 800 dwellings	=	£ 160 000
Renewal every 30 years		
Year 30 £150 × 800 × 0.0573	=	6876
Running cost per dwelling		
£150 × 800 × 9.967	=	1 196 040
Cost of mains electricity	=	free
Cost of mains gas	=	45 000
Present value cost of electric underfloor heating scheme	=	£1 407 916

(3) Gas-fired central heating

Installation £500 per dwelling	
£500 × 800 dwellings	= £400 000
Modernisation every 40 years	
Year 40 £100 × 800 × 0.0221	= 1768
Running cost per dwelling	
£75 × 800 × 9.967	= 598 020
Cost of mains electricity	= 30 000
Cost of mains gas	= free
Present value cost of gas-fired central heating scheme	= £1 029 788

(4) Solid-fuel back boiler heating

Installation and provision of fuel shed per dwelling £250	
£250 × 800 dwellings	= £200 000
Replacement of boiler every 25 years.	
Year 25 £40 × 800 × 0.0923	= 2953
Year 50 £40 × 800 × 0.0085	= 272
Replacement of radiators every 15 years.	
Year 15 £100 × 800 × 0.2393	= 19 144
Year 30 £100 × 800 × 0.0573	= 4584
Year 45 £100 × 800 × 0.0137	= 1096
Running cost per dwelling	
£100 × 800 × 9.967	= 797 360
Cost of mains electricity	= 30 000
Cost of mains gas	= 45 000
Present value cost of solid fuel back boiler heating scheme	= £1 100 409

This can be summarised as follows:

	Scheme	Present value	Annual equivalent	Annual equivalent per dwelling
(1)	District	£714 215	£71 657	£88.57
(2)	Electric	£1 407 916	£141 257	£176.57
(3)	Gas	£1 029 788	£103 320	£129.15
(4)	Solid fuel	£1 100 409	£110 405	£138.01

The annual equivalent is calculated by dividing the present value by 9.967 (the discount factor for 60 years at 10 per cent). The cost per dwelling is calculated by dividing this amount by the number of dwellings (800).

On the basis of these data, the district heating scheme is preferred as the overall economic solution. Further analysis indicates the following amounts, all discounted to present values.

	Scheme	Installation	Renewals	Running	Total
(1)	District	307 000	8535	398 680	714 215
(2)	Electric	205 000	6876	1 196 040	1 407 916
(3)	Gas	430 000	1768	598 020	1 029 788
(4)	Solid fuel	275 000	28 049	797 360	1 100 409

It can be seen that, on the basis of initial costs, the electric underfloor heating is the cheapest. However, examination of the above table shows that its running costs are the highest. Although the gas-fired central heating scheme is marginally cheaper overall than the solid fuel heating, it could not be selected on this basis alone, because future costs are unlikely to increase at an equal rate. Costs in the distant future are, incidentally, of less economic importance in the calculation than costs expended during the early years. It is also a little unusual that the radiators will survive for 40 years with a gas installation, whereas their life expectancy with solid fuel is only 15 years. Repairs and renewals can often be inconvenient, and this may be a valid objection against selecting scheme D. Although district heating is overall the most economical, and because of its low running cost is likely to be proved so in practice, it has the disadvantage that space will need to be provided on site for a boiler house. This may mean occupying valuable space on site, unsightly buildings and proneness to vandalism. Fire-safety aspects are a further factor to be taken into account in the final choice for the scheme. The district heating scheme, although the most economical, is often not favoured in practice by either users or owners, and this would also be considered when making the decision.

You have been appointed quantity surveyor by a client who proposes building a new office block for his own occupation. The architect for the development has prepared sketch drawings for two alternative designs. Although each design will satisfy the client's functional and aesthetic requirements, the capital and running costs of each scheme are different. The client asks your advice on which scheme he should choose. Using the data below:

(1) Write to the client explaining how it is possible to make an economic/financial comparison which combines both initial and recurrent costs; and

(2) Calculate both the present values and annual equivalent cost for each of the two schemes stating clearly why you have chosen a particular rate of interest for discounting; and

(3) A recently introduced external walling is considered suitable for both the alternative designs. The new walling is similar in performance to the walling shown in the sketch designs but it is 20 per cent cheaper. Show the saving that the substitution of this new walling could achieve for each of the alternatives.

General data
Life of each design: 60 years
External walling cost: £35/m^2 of walling
Ignore inflation.

Basic data
Design A
Description: Single-storey square building
Gross floor area: 10 000 m^2
Wall/floor ratio: 0.16
Construction cost: £200/m^2
Repairs: General repairs every five years equal to 10 per cent of initial
                                   capital cost. Major renovation after 30 years costing
                                   £850 000.
Lighting annual costs: £45 000
Heating annual costs: £50 000
Air conditioning
annual costs: £200 000

Design B
Description: Three-storey rectangular building with internal light wells
                                   and perimeter recessed courtyards.
Gross floor area: 11 250m^2
Wall/floor ratio: 0.48
Construction cost: £230/m^2
Repairs: General repairs every five years equal to 10 per cent of initial
                                   capital cost. Major renovation after 30 years costing
                                   £1 000 000.
Lighting annual cost: £30 000
Heating annual cost: £150 000
Air conditioning: Not required.

---

(1) It is possible to make an economic/financial comparison of buildings which combines both initial and recurrent costs, by use of appropriate discounting cash-flow techniques. Initial, periodic and regular annual payments can be converted to a common time-scale, for comparison purposes. The value of any present or future income or expenditure can be compared in this way. The alternative methods used are to either convert the sums to net present values or annual equivalent values. The advantage of carrying out a comparison in this way is to consider not just the initial cost of construction, but also the effects of alternative designs on the costs in use.

(2)(a) *Design A*
Initial construction cost
$10\,000\,m^2 \times £200/m^2$ $= 2\,000\,000$

Repairs every five years equal to 10 per cent
of the initial capital cost
Year   5   0.783526
Year 10   0.613913
Year 15   0.481017
Year 20   0.376889
Year 25   0.295303
Year 30   *
Year 35   0.181290
Year 40   0.142046
Year 45   0.111297
Year 50   0.087204
Year 55   0.068326
Year 60   *
            ‾‾‾‾‾‾‾‾
            3.140811

10 per cent $\times$ 2 000 000 $\times$ 3.140811 $=$ 628 162
Major renovation in year 30 costing £850 000
£850 000 $\times$ 0.231377 $=$ 196 670
Annual sums for
Lighting   45 000
Heating   50 000
Air conditioning   200 000
                           ‾‾‾‾‾‾‾
                           295 000 $\times$ 18.9293 $=$ 5 584 144
                           Net present value   £8 408 976

* A major renovation is required in year 30, and no general repairs will be expected. As the life of the design is 60 years, no costs for general repairs will be required in year 60.

The initial costs of construction are calculated on the basis of the gross internal floor multiplied by the superficial all-in rate of £200 per square metre. General repairs to this building are required every five years at cost of the equivalent to 10 per cent of the capital sum. The appropriate discount values have been taken from the 'present value of £1 table'. Although a regular payment for repairs is foreseen, tables do not usually provide for time intervals other than one year. The major renovation expected in year 30 of

100

£850 000 is discounted to a present value using a similar table. Annual sums for lighting, heating and air conditioning are discounted to a present value by use of the 'present value of £1 per annum table'. These sums are required for each of the 60 years. This provides us with a net present value of £8 408 976 and this can be converted to an annual equivalent cost by dividing by 18.9293 (the sum used to calculate the NPV for the annual sums).

$$\text{Annual equivalent} = \frac{£8\,408\,976}{18.9293} = £44\,230$$

(2)(b) *Design B*

Initial construction cost 11 250 m^2 × £230   =   2 587 500

Repairs every five years equal to 10 per cent of the initial capital cost.

10 per cent × 2 587 500 × 3.140811	=	812 685
Major renovation in year 30 costing £1 000 000		
£1 000 000 × 0.231377	=	231 377

Annual sums for

Lighting	30 000		
Heating	150 000		
Air conditioning	N/A		
	180 000 × 18.9293	=	3 407 274
	Net present value		£7 038 836

The whole calculation is as described previously.

$$\text{Annual equivalent} = \frac{£7\,038\,836}{18.9293} = £371\,849$$

Although scheme B provides a greater floor area, it is a much less economically efficient building in shape. This is indicated by the wall-floor ratios, and possibly by the differences in the rate per square metre, although some of this could be accounted for by a difference in the quality of work envisaged. Contrary to some opinions, the higher initial cost of scheme B also means a higher maintenance cost for that building. Therefore, because of the open-wall effect of design B, some cost savings in the annual lighting sums are achieved, and because of the greater wall area in design B a considerably larger amount of money has to be expended on the annual fuel bills. If air conditioning had been provided for in design B, this would have increased its net present value from about £7 m to almost £11 m. Although building B shows an overall cost advantage of almost £1½ m, the lack of air conditioning, which may not be considered essential today, could become a serious drawback in the future, and the building might prove difficult to sell if this was considered at some later date.

The rate of interest selected for discounting would be in accordance with prevailing rates of interest required should a company be considering a long-term loan.

(3) A reduction in the cost of external walling could be achieved as follows, based upon an approved cost of £35 per square metre with a 20 per cent saving. A saving of £7/m^2 could therefore be expected for the walling.

Design A

$$\frac{\text{Wall area}}{\text{Floor area}} = \text{wall-to-floor ratio}$$

$$\frac{\text{Wall area}}{10\,000\,\text{m}^2} = 0.16 \qquad = 1600\,\text{m}^2$$

It is unclear from the question whether or not any adjustment should be made to this area for the external doors and windows. A 20 per cent reduction has been assumed, to allow for these items.

$1600\,\text{m}^2 = 80$ per cent $\times$ £7 = £8960 saving

Design B

$$\frac{\text{Wall area}}{11\,250\,\text{m}^2} \times 0.48 \qquad\qquad = 5400\,\text{m}^2$$

$$5400\,\text{m}^2 \times 80 \text{ per cent} \times £7 = \underline{\underline{£30\,240 \text{ saving}}}$$

Both of the above are savings on the initial construction costs. It may, however, mean that an inferior material is being used that requires more maintenance, and this may have serious disadvantages for design B.

10 Development economics

A speculative developer has provided you with the following details of a proposed development of offices:

Details of complete building:

Gross floor area	$10\,000\,\text{m}^2$
Non-lettable area	22 per cent of gross floor area
Estimated rent	£60/m²
Capitalisation rate of rents	7 per cent

All outgoings to be recovered by service charge

Building contract details:

Period	18 months
Professional fees	15 per cent
Short-term finance	15 per cent
Developer's profit	12 per cent of gross development value

Land costs (including fees) £100 000
Advise your client on the allowable building costs.

This question is based upon an evaluation of probable rents in order to determine the possible funds available for building purposes. Rents are generally determined on the basis of lettable floor area. In this question, 22 per cent of the floor area is described as non-lettable and therefore as non-rentable. If this had not been given, you would have been expected to make some allowance for these areas, e.g. circulation area, etc. The normal allowance for non-lettable areas is 10–15 per cent. It could therefore be reasonably assumed that this is a prestige-type development.

Rental received

Lettable floor area = $10\,000\,\text{m}^2 \times 78$ per cent = $7800\,\text{m}^2$.
The net income per annum can therefore be calculated as:
$7800\,\text{m}^2 \times £60/\text{m}^2$ per annum = £468 000.

Gross development value

This amount must then be capitalised, i.e. converted to a current capital value. It is assumed for the purpose of this calculation that this rent will be received in perpetuity. This income is therefore multiplied by the year's purchase in perpetuity at the given percentage.

Net income	=	468 000
YP in perpetuity at 7 per cent = $\dfrac{100}{7}$ =		× 14.286
		£6 685 848

No adjustments are needed for any outgoings (i.e. repairs, rates, insurance, etc.) as these will be recovered by a separate service charge. It is further assumed that any management charges will be recovered in a similar way.

Developer's profit

The gross development value is the same as the capital value. The developer's profit is therefore calculated as 12 per cent × £6 685 848 = £802 302.

Land costs

The costs of the building site which includes professional and other fees.	=	£100 000

Short-term finance will be required on this amount until the development is complete, and then presumably let or sold. This is required for 18 months.

12 months @ 15 per cent	=	15 000
		115 000
6 months @ 15 per cent	=	8626
		£123 625

Summary

Gross development value		=	£6 685 848
Developer's profit	= £802 302		
Land cost	= £123 625		925 927
Amount of allowable building costs		=	£5 759 921

Building cost

Let B = building cost, including any adjustment for inflation. Therefore, B + finance at 15 per cent for 1½ years for half the time (the finance would be required as the work was completed. This approximately equals the full percentage for half the time) + professional fees on the building cost (assume not to be paid until completion) = the amount available for building (X).

$$= B + (B \times 0.15 \times 1\tfrac{1}{2} \times \tfrac{1}{2}) + (B \times 0.15) = X$$
$$= B + 0.1125B + 0.15B = £5\,759\,921$$
$$= 1.2625B = £5\,759\,921$$

Therefore the allowable building cost = £4 562 313

This represents approximately £456.23 per square metre for building costs (£4 562 313/10 000 m^2).

Check

It is often useful to check calculations of this type. Below is an analysis of the results.

(1) Building cost	=	£4 562 313
(2) Short-term finance at 15 per cent for 18 months £4 562 313 × 15 per cent × 1½ years × ½ (finance is required only for half the time)	=	513 261
(3) Professional fees 15 per cent × £4 562 313	=	684 347
(4) Land	=	123 625
(5) Developer's profit	=	802 302
Gross development value	=	£6 685 848

Discuss the main sources of finance available for development purposes in the private sector.

One of the largest problems facing developers and contractors, irrespective of their size and organisation, is the shortage of finance. The majority of business organisations usually commence by borrowing someone else's money on the basis that it will be repaid together with a charge for the loan. The finance for development comes from a number of alternative sources.

It may be required as a short-term loan only, to pay for land and building works from inception up to eventual disposal. Lending in this way involves greater risk than on completed buildings. For this reason, this type of finance is generally more expensive, where interest rates may be up to four points above the minimum lending rates.

Secondly, the loan may be required on a medium-term basis to finance specific expansion proposals. These loans are usually too large to be covered by short-term funding but insufficient to warrant the issue of shares. The Industrial and Commercial Finance Corporation and the Finance Corporation for Industry were formed with the main objective of investing in firms for periods up to seven years.

Thirdly, the finance may be required on a long-term basis for periods in excess of ten years. The traditional method of providing this finance is by means of a mortgage. It has been suggested that insurance companies and pension funds dominate the commercial and industrial sector, whereas the building societies have the largest share in the private house building market.

The cost of finance is of major importance in any decisions regarding borrowing. Supply and demand, the levels of inflation, the time preference factor and the risk associated with the loan are all considerations influencing the rates of interest. The most critical, however, when negotiating terms for finance is the risk element. Construction is regarded as a high-risk activity, and the numbers of bankruptcies support this opinion. Interest rates charged to building contractors, therefore, tend to be higher than the average, and the smaller company tends to fare even worse.

The following are the main sources of finance that are available for development purposes.

Owner's capital

This includes retained earnings in the form of profits, and is the most economical source should it be available. The use of trading funds, deferred expenses for goods and materials or money set aside for taxation purposes may also be available in the short term.

Bank overdraft

This is unlikely to be available as a source of finance for building development. Its main use is for the firm's general running expenses or for short-term bridging purposes. High rates of interest are generally charged for overdrafts.

Loans

This is similar to an overdraft but is available on a much longer-term basis. It is common for the smaller firm to obtain this form of finance from the bank, whereas a large organisation may choose an insurance company or similar financial organisation. Special financial institutions to help industry have been created, such as ICFC (Industrial and Commercial Finance Corporation) which may be approached, or ventures of a special type could find support from organisations such as the National Enterprise Board. In addition it may be possible for firms to obtain loans from other government funds at lower rates of interest than money raised in the commercial market.

Shares

Property companies are able to raise capital by selling shares to purchasers who then receive a share of the profits when distributed. There are several different types of share available that offer variable rates of return on the investment and different types of security. Ordinary shares are often known as equity shares. These entitle their owners to the remainder of the profits after the dividends of preference shareholders have been met. They do not therefore carry a fixed rate of interest. Should the company enter into liquidation, the ordinary shareholders will receive their amounts invested only after the claims of creditors, debenture holders and preference shareholders have been settled.

Preference shares carry a fixed rate of interest and have to be paid in full before any dividend is paid to the holders of ordinary shares. Cumulative preference shares are an even safer form of investment offering their holders protection against bad years. The holders of such shares have the right to carry forward unpaid amounts of dividends to the following years. Debentures are another way by which a company may raise capital. These are essentially loans to the company and do not allow their holders to vote. They involve less risk than shares because they carry a fixed rate of interest which must be paid irrespective of whether the company makes a profit or a loss.

Hire purchase and leasing

If a firm has insufficient capital for both equipment and development, it can obtain the former by hire purchase, which is in effect a loan, and so release its capital for development purposes. In other circumstances the firm may choose to lease the equipment for a minimum period, with an option to purchase at the end of the time period. The leasing of equipment often incorporates maintenance agreements and taxation advantages.

Instalment finance

The majority of major building works are paid for on the basis of interim payments. The price of the project is therefore paid for on an instalment basis, usually representing 90 per cent of the value of the work complete. Payment in this way helps to reduce the borrowing requirements of the contractor. The developer, where he is not the contractor, may be able to offset these sums by either forward selling or pre-selling methods, where monies are received in advance of completion.

Describe the factors that a developer will consider when selecting a suitable site for building purposes.

There is a wide range of considerations influencing the development of a building site. The location of the site for public authority development will often be dictated by the social needs of the area. The development of industry must be closely followed by that of housing which in turn requires schools, shopping facilities, health care, etc. A developer who has available a selection of building sites for development will make his choice after considering the following factors.

Type of development

The type of development anticipated will need to be considered. A large flat site, for example, may be favoured for industrial-type buildings whereas an undulating site may provide more scope for design, and the creation of more pleasant conditions for housing purposes. Decisions made under this heading will also relate to the quantity and quality of accommodation to be provided, the numbers and size of individual units together with estate road layout, the amounts of open spaces required and the requirements for car parking. These decisions will ultimately be made by the client on the basis of a variety of professional advice, including a description of the site, from which the client will seek his optimum design. Economic consideration will be a major influence, although there can be many examples chosen to show that prestige and personal preference may overrule this factor.

Physical factors

Each site has its own characteristics which have an important influence on its suitability for development. The size of the site will be particularly important. This may vary from a single housing plot to many acres available for large-scale development. Ground conditions will be a factor that can substantially influence constructional costs. Ground offering a poor or dubious load-bearing capacity can, in addition to necessitating expensive foundations, create site problems. Such sites may only be selected for their locational aspects or because no other site is available. Steeply-sloping sites may result in expensive earthworks, and additional expenditure will be required to remove obstructions such as derelict buildings or structures below ground. In some cases it may be necessary to redirect water courses or install some form of land drainage before work can commence.

Planning controls

Planning permission is required for most forms of private development, and is obtained from the local planning authority in the prescribed manner. Permission may be granted conditionally or without any special restrictions, or it can be refused, in which case the owner can appeal for a decision from the minister. Outline approval can be sought, and this is especially useful when the purchase of a site is under consideration. The location of the site may determine its permitted uses, although planning permission will still be required. The use of land can often severely influence its valuation in the market, and these will be major factors for the developer to consider. The planning proposal will be restricted to a permitted maximum density to which it can be developed, and may need to show the requirements for landscaping and car parking facilities. In some circumstances existing buildings which are of special architectural or historic interest cannot be demolished, extended, or altered, and this may make the site unattractive for development purposes. Other statutory requirements may also be in force; for example, the necessity to obtain an Industrial Development Certificate before building work can commence.

Legal considerations

Land can be subject to various legal restrictions that can have the effect of making development more expensive or even impossible. The two main types of restriction on development are classified as either restrictive covenants or easements. Restrictive covenants impose conditions which govern the use of the land. They generally restrict the developer in the way that he can use the land. An easement is a privilege in law which one owner has in the property of another. The most common easements relating to building development are: the right of light, right of support, right of way and right of drainage. Land subject to easements is normally reduced in value since it restricts the owner's full use and enjoyment of the site. Other legal aspects that the developer will consider are those of tenure relating to freehold and leasehold.

Locational aspects

The location of the site will be influenced by the type of development contemplated. The main factors the developer will be concerned with here will be satisfactory access to the site and the availability of mains services. It is essential for some sites, particularly those required for industrial development, to be close to major highways with good service roads.

Describe the taxation influences affecting the provision of capital building works.

All companies are subject to assessment by the Inland Revenue, and the taxation levied can have an important effect upon cash flow. It is therefore important to take this into account when appraising projects, since tax can have the effect of turning apparently profitable projects into loss-makers. Taxation rates and allowances are subject to changes imposed by governments of all political persuasions. The Finance Act of 1965 included the concept of Corporation Tax payable by companies but not by local authorities. The tax payable is calculated on the basis of income received, but relief is allowed for certain expenditure such as repairs and maintenance of buildings.

Items of capital expenditure on new or enlarged buildings are generally not deductable except in certain special cases. Depreciation allowances, for example, were introduced in 1945 for all types of industrial building. These allowances vary from time to time, but can include an initial allowance and an annual writing-down allowance. In 1974 these amounts were 40 and 4 per cent respectively for these types of building. The cost of the land on which the building stands is not allowable, but any costs for site clearance or preparation are an allowable deduction.

It may seem unreasonable that plant and machinery can claim either the full allowance initially or a reduced amount and then claim an annual writing-down allowance of 25 per cent, whereas buildings cannot. However, this is probably because buildings appreciate in value, whereas plant and machinery do not. It could be argued, however, that providing comparable allowances for buildings would create more work for the building industry. The current rules may also encourage firms to spend less initially, when no tax allowance is deductable, and more on repairs and maintenance which are allowable items against expected profits.

In order to encourage industrial premises to save energy, special measures were intrduced in 1974 to provide a full allowance initially on the costs of thermal insulation to industrial buildings.

In addition to plant and machinery, furniture and fittings and other office equipment for any type of business premises can also be included as capital allowances.

Tax concessions may also be given in the form of grants to encourage capital development of certain types of building in specified areas. The types of development for which grants may be available include factory buildings, tourism, leisure, conservation and housing, and the work can comprise new work or rehabilitation. The size of the grant can vary between 20 and 25 per cent, depending upon the status of the area concerned which may be described as a special development area, development area or intermediate area. Grants can be obtained from one of the regional offices of the Department of Trade and Industry. The allowable cost will not normally include the cost of the site, but will include any site preparation prior to building work. There may also be the possibility of obtaining loans on favourable terms for development from the European Investment Bank which supplies finance from the European Community Fund.

An important consideration affecting the worth of a grant to a developer is the time when it is received, and whether it can be paid in advance of the project or only by a reimbursement arrangement. The same principle also needs to be applied to tax payments, and it is worth noting that corporation tax is normally due nine months after the end of the accounting period.

There is therefore a wide variation of taxation relief applicable to building expenditure, ranging from no relief in the normal case, through to some relief for industrial premises and attractive allowances, depending upon the status of the area of the site location. Maintenance expenditure is a wholly deductible tax allowance. A developer, therefore, when deciding either to rebuild or simply maintain his existing premises, needs to take these considerations into account.

Other forms of financial inducement may be available that can affect the investment decision. Subsidies may be payable for employees, or low-rent accommodation may be provided by a local authority to entice industrialists into a particular location. This latter condition normally runs only for a limited number of years, whereas the former is generally subject to a political policy decision.

The forms of taxation affecting capital works therefore include: corporation tax, development land tax, value added tax, Stamp Duty, rates and capital gains tax. In addition, government may offer grants or other incentives to encourage building work of certain types in certain parts of the country.

Describe the alternative methods that can be used for the valuation of land and property.

Valuations of land and property are usually undertaken by the valuation surveyor for a number of different purposes. The purpose of the valuation will affect the assessment of its value, and this may differ because of the assumptions made and also because they are only estimates of value anyway. Valuations are required for statutory purposes in order to assess capital transfer tax, or when a public body seeks to acquire land or property by means of compulsory purchase. A valuation may also be necessary when a purchaser such as an insurance company or pension fund wants to invest its capital. It may also be needed during the sale and purchase of property, in connection with a mortgage loan or for determining an auction reserve. A number of alternative methods can be used to estimate either the capital value or the rental value of an interest in land or property. Values can vary considerably, depending upon the location nationally or even within a small area.

The comparative method

This is the most popular method used for valuation purposes. Its main use is in connection with residential property where direct comparisons can be made against other types of property on the open market. The method is only reliable, however, where there are efficient records of many recent transactions and the properties are in the same area. Other factors that influence the valuation are: the similarity of properties in design, size and condition and the legal interest. A stable market, and economic factors such as lending rates, also affect the reliability of the valuation.

The contractor's method

The basis of this method is to suggest that the value of a property is equivalent to the cost of erecting the buildings, together with the cost of the site. It is, however, an unsound assumption since value is determined not by cost but by the amount which prospective purchasers are prepared to pay. Its main use is in connection with valuations for insurance purposes.

The residual method

This method is used in those circumstances where the value of a property can be increased after carrying out development work. For example, an old house may be capable of conversion into flats, when its best potential can be realised. The building is valued on the basis of its future worth after conversion, and the costs of this work together with developer's costs are then deducted. The resulting sum is the value of the property in its original state and is known as its residual value.

The profits or accounts method

Almost all types of property are capable of producing an income under certain conditions, and a relationship will exist between this and the capital value of the property. It is more appropriate to commercial premises such as hotels, shops and leisure projects than domestic premises. The usual approach is to estimate the gross earnings, deduct expenses and the balance remaining then represents the amount available for payment of rents. This can then be converted into a capital sum.

The investment method

This method can also be used in those circumstances where the property produces an income. The income expected must be comparable with that which could be earned by investing the capital elsewhere. In considering alternative investment possibilities, factors such as security values, ease of realisation, costs of purchase and selling, and any tax liability will influence competing proposals. The principal investors are pension funds, insurance companies, property companies, historic owners, local authorities and government agencies.

Apart from the profits method, all the above methods are useful for estimating capital values, whereas the residual method and investment method are not really suitable for the determination of rental value. The demand for a particular type of landed property will be influenced by changes in: the size of population, methods of communication, standards of living and society in general.

Describe how inflation, interest rates and taxation are allowed for in investment appraisal calculations.

Those responsible for the evaluation of the financial aspects of design decisions in the construction industry have realised that comparisons based solely upon the initial building costs are no longer adequate. The costs throughout the life of the building's use must also be taken into account. Furthermore it is insufficient simply to add these amounts together, since their expenditures are in different time-scales. The technique used to convert these different amounts into comparable values is known as discounted cash flow analysis. The principle of this concept, of the time value of money, is a 'rate of time preference'. This means that money which arises in the near future is preferred to money which arises in the far future.

Inflation

Inflation may be described as either general inflation, in which case it affects a whole range of items, or special inflation, in which case it relates only to particular goods or materials. Inflation can have an important effect upon the financial consequences of alternative design solutions.

Two alternative approaches can be adopted to deal with the problem of inflation in an economic appraisal calculation. Although the first method is generally preferred in practice, some consideration should be given to the possible differences in the way that inflation may affect various building materials, processes and systems.

(1) The first alternative is to ignore inflation on the assumption that it is impossible to forecast it, and that in real terms there will be relatively little change in comparative values. Thus in relation to development, a future rise in money terms of the costs of building is likely to be matched by a similar rise in money terms of values. It is therefore reasonable and realistic to work in terms of today's costs and today's values. An objection to this theory is that the values of buildings tend to move rather erratically, whereas with the costs of buildings the increases are much more gradual.

(2) The alternative approach is to attempt to take account of inflation in the financial appraisal. The evidence from market expectations coupled with intuitive judgement and prevailing economic conditions can be used to assess possible changes in actual terms.

Interest rates

The selection of an interest rate for discounting relates to the real cost of finance. In the immediate future this is difficult to assess, and in calculations over the 60-year life of a building its prediction is impossible. However, the rate of interest is not so important or critical for sums received or expended at some time in the future. The effect of using too high a discount rate throughout is to favour those projects with low initial costs and high running costs. Using too low a discount rate produces the opposite effect. The discount rate selected should therefore properly reflect the organisation's opportunity cost of capital. This is represented by the market interest rate. However, this rate may be adjusted depending upon the level of risk and uncertainty associated with the project.

Taxation

Because the objective of financial appraisal is to minimise the total life-cycle cost, all cash flows of whatever type must be included. An organisation will only be concerned with actual cash flows of a project. These cash flows must therefore take into account the appropriate taxation charges to be levied and the reliefs that may be available. They must also take into account the relevant time when such payments fall due or when such sums become receivable. There is a wide variation of fiscal relief against which building cost expenditure can be claimed, but the matter is complicated because such relief is often under review and revision. It has often been argued that whilst maintenance expenditure is wholly allowable against taxation, capital expenditure generally is not and this results in the former being comparatively less expensive.

Examination technique

It cannot be overemphasised that lack of knowledge cannot be replaced by some miracle technique in order to pass an examination. Students who believe that they can waffle or fudge their way through are only deceiving themselves. It is, however, true to say that by approaching the examination in a particular way, a marginal fail can be converted into a pass, or a mediocre mark can become one of substance. Correct study and preparation are the essentials of any examination and students should aim to secure as high a mark as possible by alerting themselves to questions of any eventuality. It is not the intention to mention book titles of 'How to pass examinations'; needless to say that they do exist. Their mottoes are, however, simple and straightforward: if you want to pass, you must study. Possibly by the time students reach the level of the questions in this book, they will already be at a final level of ordinary degrees or professional institutions examinations. They will already have had the daunting experience of sitting in an examination hall. Two other avenues that can be usefully explored in the studying process are those of memory training and rapid reading. They have been tried and tested, and in many cases have achieved the desired results; but they are, I must stress, no substitute for studying subject matter. They can at best assist students in their examination performance. Students should therefore try to ensure that they have covered the syllabus content as fully as possible, in order to ensure that no question that appears on the examination paper comes as a complete surprise.

The night before the examination might be usefully spent revising those last-minute details, but that is its limit. If you don't know the subject matter before then, this last evening isn't really going to help a great deal. Banking on 'luck' is not a course of action that I would advocate, although it might be argued that in those marginal situations it can result in a pass or a fail. Students really need to arrive as fresh as possible to the examination hall complete with all their wits about them.

It is certainly useful to look at the previous year's examination questions for several reasons. First, they provide some indication of the type and standard of question to be expected. The preceding years' questions do not often have a radical approach, even where a new examiner may have been appointed. The distribution of marks, compulsory questions and amount of choice usually varies only slightly from one year to the next, so that previous years' papers should provide a good guide and show any trends in their design. Secondly, it may be possible to detect some pattern in the questions asked. One may be able to deduce that this question or that question appears to be a likely one for this year, since it was some years since such a question was asked. Examiners obviously look back over previous years' questions, but some students seem to be good at predicting a pattern of questions that examiners are unaware of! However, these predictions, like our weather forecasts, are often wrong! It is more appropriate to subdivide the syllabus into sections, and then work on questions that might occur from these groups. Of course, where one is fortunate to know the examiner (who is also possibly the lecturer), it is sometimes possible to detect pet themes or interests, and these may then be appropriate topics for examination. Once the subject matter has been fully studied it is a good approach to spend time answering previous years' questions, sometimes timing yourself as a further test. This procedure should assist with revision and also help you to prepare for examination conditions.

Where examiners produce reports on the questions they have set and the answers that they have received, these can be of great assistance to prospective students. They provide an indication of the answer expected, together with comments upon the student's performance. The majority of the professional institutions provide this service for their own internal use, and are also prepared to offer it to students at a reasonable charge. The reports often suggest that students lose valuable marks through the poor organisation of their examination answer scripts. The following suggestions are made as a method of improving candidate's performance.

(1) Read through the paper quickly and carefully note the examiner's requirements about the number of questions to be answered, the necessity of any compulsory question and other general instructions. Candidates should be aware beforehand which standard books, publications or mathematical tables they will be allowed to use for reference, and which of these they should provide themselves.

(2) The question paper may be in parts or sections, in which case special instructions may apply to the different sections. Unless otherwise stated, it should be assumed that all questions carry equal marks and will therefore be of proportional worth, and require equal time for the answer.

(3) Because of the time required for preparatory work before starting to answer the questions, and the time required at the end of the examination for a general reading-through of answers, some adjustment needs to be made on the actual time allowed for each question. For example, in a three-hour examination in which candidates have to answer five equal questions, there is only about 30 minutes to devote to each question.

(4) Decide on the questions you find the easiest and then number them accordingly. If you have difficulty in choosing your final question, then leave this decision until you have answered question four. Always attempt the required number of questions for the reason stated later. Answering the easiest question first will get you off to a good start and increase your confidence.

(5) Where a question requires the use of a formula, write this down immediately, just in case you forget it later!

(6) Read each question carefully, at least twice so that there is no doubt about what the examiner requires. Be prepared to answer the question fully, but try to avoid including in your answer material that is irrelevant. List on rough paper the major points that you will want to cover in your answer. Remember that you will only obtain marks for your answer to that question, and not for a good answer to a question that has not been asked.

(7) If you find yourself running short of your allotted time before completing the answer, try to bring it to some reasonable conclusion. If the opposite is true, do not waste your time trying to 'pad' out an answer, because no marks are given for waffle!

(8) If you find yourself so short of time that you are unable to attempt the final question properly, instead try to list all the main points which would be included in a full answer. In this way you should be awarded some marks.

(9) When examiners set a question paper they are often required to provide their answer and a schedule of how the marks will be distributed. A typical example of this is shown towards the end of this section. Generally, marks can be awarded for a variety of purposes such as: presentation of work, procedure used, accuracy of results, knowledge of subject matter, completeness of answer etc. Although the marks may be awarded in varying proportions according to the subject concerned, the following will provide a guide.

Presentation and procedures	6–10 per cent
Knowledge of subject	60–80 per cent
Completeness of answer	20–30 per cent

(10) Remember that it is always easy to pick up the first few marks to any question by showing the examiner that you understand the principles involved. Conversely it is extremely difficult to collect the last few marks required for a perfect answer.

(11) Candidates with a good knowledge of the subject matter who provide an answer with a high standard of presentation are likely to gain very good marks even if they may have been unable to finish all of the question.

(12) Approximately quarter of an hour from the end of the examination it is a good practice to read through your answers to check spelling, grammar and punctuation. You may also feel that further points need to be included, and reading over should help you with this aspect.

(13) Before releasing your answer book, put all of the pages in the proper order, making sure your name or number (if this is all that has been requested) is on every individual sheet of paper.

(14) Once the examination is concluded and you have left the hall, it will be time for a post-mortem. Chances are, you will take part in this, since most of us like to compare answers. One thing, however, that you should not do is to worry about how badly you might have done, because it is too late to do anything about it now, and there is no point in making yourself miserable.

Marking scheme

The following is a typical example of how an examiner might prepare his marking scheme. It is precise enough to assist other examiners to mark the work should this be necessary, although it does not eliminate the possibility of awarding some marks on a purely subjective basis. For the majority of important examinations, model answers and marking schemes will be required. Because they will be read by other examiners, these have the advantage of ensuring that question means what the examiner intended and also that an adequate answer is available. The marking scheme below refers to the question and answer on page 24, and is based upon a total allocation of 25 marks.

Description of cost model	4
Construction of cost model	
Type of model	2
Collection of data	2
Selection of technique	2
Computer application	2
Analysis of model	2
Testing of model	2
Model in-use	2
Advantages and disadvantages	7
	25 marks

Revision questions

(1)(a) What do you understand by 'value for money' from the building owner's point of view?

(b) List the criteria which you consider would be suitable for the measurement of value for money in building; discuss these criteria and consider any difficulties that might be encountered in such measurement.

(2) Discuss the problems of data collection, analysis and interpretation in connection with a costs-in-use study for a proposed old people's home.

(3) Distinguish between the economic life and structural life of buildings and explain their significance in the costing of building designs. Discuss the case for securing maximum adaptability in building designs, outlining the practical difficulties of implementing such a policy.

(4)(a) Describe the sources from which a quantity surveyor may obtain data for preparing approximate estimates for building works. Clearly summarise the merits of each source.

(b) Show by examples how cost data can be updated to current costs and predicted to future costs. Discuss the adjustments you would make for such factors as market influences.

(5) Distinguish between approximate estimating and cost planning.

Describe the procedure for cost checking during the detailed design stage and the corrective actions that may have to be taken.

(6) 'The points to be taken into account when engaged in cost studies on (a) buildings held as an investment, (b) buildings held as a factor of production vary in importance.'

List the points referred to and discuss how the importance of each is established for building types (a) and (b).

(7) Discuss the factors you would take into account when giving your client cost advice at the feasibility stage of the design process. Assume that tenders are to be obtained using limited competition and traditional documentation.

(8) Financial advice given by building economists at the design stage of a project tends not to reflect the effect of the design solution on the method of construction.

Discuss.

(9) During the design stage of a project new information impingeing upon the planned cost of the building is constantly coming to the notice of the quantity surveyor from many different sources and through a variety of media. List eight different sources of such information and discuss briefly the action he should take in each case to ensure that the cost control function is carried out efficiently.

(10) The quantity surveyor often needs to adjust cost data to current and future price levels. Describe the methods used, the problems encountered and how they may be overcome.

(11) Considerable time and expense can be spent in the preparation of amplified cost analyses of buildings. Discuss the uses of such analyses and their benefits and shortcomings, and consider whether the information obtained justifies the effort incurred. Suggest any changes you would like to see in the approach or format.

(12) 'In buildings of a life span of not more than ten years it is more economical to have low initial cost and high maintenance costs.' Discuss the validity of this statement.

(13) High rates of short-term finance and rising building costs are currently seriously affecting house building.

   Discuss, using a calculation to illustrate your answer, the effect a delay to a contract may have on the final total cost of a project to construct a small estate of 25 houses with an approximate sale price of £40 000 each.

(14) A building which is to be pulled down in 25 years time requires repainting now and will require further repainting every five years until demolition. The cost of each repainting is estimated at £250. In ten years time £1500 is to be spent on alterations. £100 will be spent at the end of each year for sundry repairs. What sum must be set aside now to pay for all this work if the rate of interest that can be obtained on investment is 10 per cent? (The effect of taxation is to be ignored.)

(15) How would you define an economic design solution and to what extent do you consider that statutory cost limits affect the opportunity to obtain such a solution?

(16) Costs in use can be considered to include all the costs incurred in erecting, occupying, maintaining and ultimately demolishing a building.
(a) Discuss how decisions at design stage can affect costs in use;
(b) What are the problems encountered when making costs-in-use comparisons of alternative design solutions?

(17) The cost of providing a unit in a building, such as a bed space in a hospital or a pupil in a school at any one point in time, varies from project to project. Summarise the reasons why this should be the case.

(18) You are appointed quantity surveyor on a project to fit out a five-storey speculative office shell of 5000 m² lettable floor area for a large firm of solicitors, as tenant-occupiers. The tenants have negotiated a six-months rent-free period commencing in three months time. Making assumptions about specification requirements, write a letter to the client advising on his likely capital commitment and the most appropriate form of contractual procedure.

(19) Prepare a cost target for external walling in a proposed four-storey block of flats based on a cost analysis of the tender for a three-storey block of flats containing the following data:

Cost of external walling in existing building/m²
of gross floor area   = £7.30
External wall area of existing building/
  Gross floor area   = £0.75
Price level index at analysis tender date   = £273

Current price level index   = £312
Gross floor area of proposed building   = $2300\,m^2$
External wall area of proposed building   = $1740\,m^2$
The ratio of windows to net external wall is assumed to be constant in both buildings.

(20) A manufacturer has recently obtained the production rights for a new product for which he considers there will be a demand over the next 10 years. He therefore requires new premises to be constructed on land which he owns. Two alternatives are under consideration:

(a) **Prefabricated Buildings**

Construction time	6 months
Total initial cost	£100 000
Maintenance cost	£10 000 per annum
Repairs every 5th year	£4 000
Major works at 10th year	£20 000
Life of building	20 years

(b)

Construction time	18 months
Total initial cost	£120 000
Maintenance cost	£5 000 per annum
Life of building	40 years

The manufacturer pays corporation tax @ 52 per cent and has a cost of capital after tax of 5 per cent.

Prepare a calculation to appraise the situation and list fully your advice to your client, making and listing any necessary assumptions.(*Note:* an answer in report form is not required.)

(21) Explain the basic concept of cost in use and outline the difficulties in relation to the items listed below and how these are overcome:
(a) An appropriate discounting rate.
(b) Provision for sinking funds.
(c) Taxation allowance for future maintenance costs.
(d) Ministry grants for initial capital expenditure in assisted areas,
(e) Inflation of future costs.

(22) 'In house building repetition leads to an increase in productivity. The increase is not maintained when the design of house type changes.'
Comment on this statement.

(23) Describe the advantages and disadvantages of the BCIS and CI/SfB tables of elements in the context of design cost control.

(24) Discuss how economies incorporated by the Architect in the design can be effectively communicated by the Bills of Quantities to the Contractor for tender purposes.

(25) Describe in detail a 'Preliminary Cost Plan' and explain the minimum information which is essential for its preparation. State which items are of cost significance and will, in your opinion, require careful cost checking during the design stage.

(26)(a) Discuss the major reasons for the increasing realisation of the need for cost control during the pre-contract stages of building design.

(b) Give examples of how you would prepare a cost plan for the following elements:

(i) foundations;

(ii) structural frame;

(iii) external cladding;

(iv) mechanical services; and

(v) joinery fittings.

(27) There are different ways of ensuring that building contracts are let at competitive prices.

Discuss the role of competition in the cost control function making reference to the other important facets and give examples of three situations in which formal competition between building contractors (or sub-contractors) might be of little significance in the overall context.

(28) When consulted on comparative building costs for alternative designs for an office scheme you have been requested to take annual running and maintenance costs into account.

Describe how you would analyse the annual costs of both schemes, giving likely sources of data and, using appropriate figures, show how the comparison would be expressed in your report. (N.B. For the purposes of this answer you are *not* required to write a full report and the taxation aspect can be ignored.)

(29) You have been asked to construct an index for use in updating the cost information in the library of cost analyses in a large private practice.

Explain how you would go about this task.

(30) Discuss those factors which influence the accuracy of the process of Cost Planning.

(31)(a) Discuss the effect that height and plan shape have on the total cost of a building.

(b) How might constraints concerning:

(i) use of a building; and

(ii) time for completion of a building;

be reflected in the form of construction chosen and the cost of construction?

(32) 'The only significant result of employing a quantity surveyor is to add about 3 per cent to the cost of a project'. Discuss this statement in the context of a Q.S. appointment simply to prepare bills of quantities and to carry out basic final account duties i.e. measurement and valuation of variations and valuation for the interim and final certificates.

(33) Explain the factors which you would take into account when advising a property owner whether to refurbish a building, demolish it and redevelop the site or do nothing other than essential repairs.

(34) Discuss and compare the economics of any four different methods of heating a speculative light industrial building.

(35) A quantity surveyor is appointed to carry out cost control of a new warehouse which will be occupied by the Building Employer as a major centre of his operations. Discuss the likely significance of this appointment with regard to:
(a) the total overhead costs of the occupier's trading operations,
(b) the performance of the buildings,
(c) the profit margin of the appointed building contractor stating the facets of cost control which are of the greatest significance in each case.

(36) It is often said that the first estimate given to a client is the only one he ever remembers. Assuming this to have a foundation in truth, discuss steps which a quantity surveyor can take to prevent dissatisfaction and recrimination by the client at the final cost of his project.

(37) What do you understand by the term 'cost-sensitive element'?
Illustrate with examples how knowledge of this aspect of building economics might be usefully applied in the design of an office building where Town Planning requirements are flexible, building budget per unit of floor area is fairly stringent and the ground has low bearing capacity.

(38) A recent survey has shown fairly conclusively that construction costs of most types of building in the USA are substantially less than in the UK at current rates of exchange. Given that the role of the professional quantity surveyor as we know it is virtually non-existent in the USA, what significance do you see in these findings and what explanation can you give for the differences in economic performance?

(39) Discuss the cost-sensitivity of each of the following elements:
(a) a church roof;
(b) foundations of a multi-storey block of flats;
(c) wall finishes in a local authority two-storey housing scheme;
(d) heating installation in a publisher's warehouse;
(e) floor finishes in a speculative office building;
(f) external walls of a large detached bungalow.

(40) Discuss the issues in establishing a cost limit for a local authority old persons' home consistent with the other demands on the authority's resources.

(41) Explain the difference between the BCIS 'general building cost index' and BCIS 'tender price index'.
Explain how you would update a cost analysis from 1971 (second quarter) to 1981 (third quarter).
To what matters should you have particular regard when using this analysis for cost planning purposes?

(42) A site has recently been purchased by a developer for £50 000 (including all fees) with planning permission for the erection of houses. Tenders have been received from two contractors on a design-and-construct package deal for houses which have an estimated sale price, excluding fees, of £893 000 at present-day prices. Both tenders are on the basis of interim monthly payments and commencement of works on site within three months from receipt by the developer of tenders. Short-term finance has been arranged at 15 per cent per annum. The developer estimates that house prices will rise by 12 per cent during the first year and stabilise at that level during the following year.

121

Details of the tenders are as follows:

(a) **Tender 1**

    Price £700 000   Completion 12 months.

(b) **Tender 2**

    Price £620 000   Completion 18 months.

Advise the developer which tender to accept, giving reasons.

Bibliography

Ashworth, A. & Skitmore, M.	Accuracy in Estimating. 1982 CIOB.
Barrett, F. R.	Cost Value Reconciliation. 1981 CIOB.
Bathurst, P. E. & Butler, D. A.	Building Cost Control Techniques and Economics. 2 edn. 1980 Heineman.
Bennett, J.	Cost Planning and Computers. 1981 HMSO.
Brandon, P. S.	Building Cost Techniques. New Directions. 1982 Spon.
Browning, C.	Building Economics and Cost Planning. Batsford.
Buchanan, J.	Cost Models for Estimating. 1972 RICS.
Davis, Belfield & Everest	Spons Architect and Builders Price Book. 1982 Spon.
Dent, C.	Construction Cost Appraisal. 1971 Godwin.
Ferry, D. J. & Brandon, P. S.	Cost Planning of Buildings. 1980 Granada.
Gobourne, J.	Site Cost Control in the Construction Industry. 1982 Butterworth.
Hillebrandt, P. M.	Economic Theory and the Construction Industry. 1977 Macmillan.
Nisbet, J.	Estimating and Cost Control. 1961 Batsford.
Pilcher, R.	Appraisal and Control of Project Costs. 1973 McGraw-Hill.
Saunt, T. J.	Revision Notes on Building Economics. 1975 Butterworth.
Seeley, I. H.	Building Economics. 1979 Macmillan.
Southwell, J.	Total Building Cost Appraisal. 1967 RICS.
Southwell, J.	Building Cost Forecasting. 1971 RICS.
Stone, P. A.	Building Economy. 1976 Pergamon.
Stone, P. A.	Building Design Evaluation, Costs in Use. 1968 Spon.
Turin, D. A.	Aspects of the Economics of Construction. 1975 Godwin.

| Tysoe, A. | Construction Cost and Price Indices: Description and Use. 1981 Spon. |
| Ward & Lichfield | Cost Control in Design and Construction. 1980 McGraw-Hill. |

Cost Control in Building Design. 1974 HMSO.

Cost in Use – a Study of 24 Crown Office Buildings. 1972 HMSO.

Chartered Quantity Surveyors and the Microcomputer. 1981 RICS.

Construction Economics: The International Role of the Chartered Quantity Surveyor. 1977 RICS.

Building Bulletin 4: Cost Study. 1972 HMSO.

An Introduction to Cost Planning. 1976 RICS.

Engineering Economics. 1979 ICE.

Costs in Use, Elemental Tables. 1977 HMSO.

Building Cost Information Service. RICS.

Building Maintenance Cost Information Service. RICS.